T0380265

# THROUGH
# THE
# RED
# DOOR

*The Church of the Advocate*
*A narrative collection of its people, history, and spirit*
*1997 - 2022*

## DENA BEARL WHALEN

WESTBOW
P R E S S®
A DIVISION OF THOMAS NELSON
& ZONDERVAN

WestBow Press books may be ordered through booksellers or by contacting:

WestBow Press
A Division of Thomas Nelson & Zondervan
1663 Liberty Drive
Bloomington, IN 47403
www.westbowpress.com
844-714-3454

Because of the dynamic nature of the Internet, any web addresses or links contained in this book may have changed since publication and may no longer be valid. The views expressed in this work are solely those of the author and do not necessarily reflect the views of the publisher, and the publisher hereby disclaims any responsibility for them.

Any people depicted in stock imagery provided by Getty Images are models, and such images are being used for illustrative purposes only. Certain stock imagery © Getty Images.

Scripture quotations are taken from the New Revised Standard Version Bible, copyright 1989, Division of Christian Education of the National Council of the Churches of Christ in the United States of America. Used by permission. All rights reserved.

ISBN: 979-8-3850-2508-4 (sc)
ISBN: 979-8-3850-2509-1 (e)

Library of Congress Control Number: 2024909581

Print information available on the last page.

WestBow Press rev. date: 05/16/2024

To my husband Gary for his unwavering encouragement and love.
To our God of hope, who continues to kindle in the Church the
fire of transformative Love.

# CONTENTS

# CONTENTS

# FOREWORD

Jesus was homeless, too.

Through the Red Door is a story, told in many voices, about a faith community which started out with a priest and deacon who went out to meet Jesus on the streets of Asheville, North Carolina. Their card table set up in a central park with communion and peanut butter sandwiches grew into one of the earliest congregations in a movement begun in the 1990's. The Church of the Advocate is now one of 200 affiliates world-wide, each of which is unique, and all of which are grounded in welcome, haven and spiritual support for people living without the safety and security of permanent housing.

The "mother" street ministry – Boston's common cathedral - emerged out of my own spiritual journey. In recovery from conditions which frequently plague people who are homeless, I found myself moved to hang out on park benches and in subway stations and train tunnels. At first, I just talked with people who were willing to talk. Sometimes I'd bring coffee or a sandwich. I was looking for God in whomever I met. Making genuine connection was my hope.

Eventually, after my ordination to the priesthood, I wanted to share eucharist with some of the folks I'd gotten to know. On a Christmas morning, I put the makings of eucharist in my backpack and headed to a train station in Boston where many folks kept warm and dry when other locations were closed. A friend joined me and brought soup, which we all enjoyed after that first simple communion together. We met for liturgy and soup in the South Station every Sunday after that.

On Easter morning, we left our enclosed space and gathered around a folding table under a tree on busy Boston Common. The next day, our photograph was in "The Boston Herald," and the word was out. Each week afterwards new people arrived – those who lived on the street and those who came from homes; some seeking us out intentionally and others discovering us as they walked through the park.

We had not planned for anything like this, but a church without walls was growing under that tree. Every week we learned anew what it means to be loved by God and by one another – just as we are - and not as we used to be or could be. What fed us was the joy and revelation of experiencing church, alive, wherever people are, made of the shards of real life and big enough to welcome all: the bloody faces, the raw truth, the seizures and the squabbling, the despair and the ecstasy.

This account of the particular life and development of the Church of the Advocate raises themes heard throughout the network of street ministries: The way in which singular spiritual journeys can lead to surprising, new community; the relief and redemption of being known by name and respected as God's own; the questioning of the function and meaning of "church" and "charity;" the power of communities of forgiveness, accompaniment and celebration.

You'll also read about the resistance street ministries experience. When I was first engaged in street ministry, not everyone saw it as a priestly ministry. Some on the street reminded me that even doing good can be hustle. Funding is a chronic challenge, as is space – whether outdoors or indoors. Many people simply didn't understand that we were not gathered to solve anything, to convert or to save – but to love God and neighbor as ourselves.

I'm so glad a copy of Through the Red Door has landed in your hands. In addition to being an inspiring portrait of a vital street ministry in Asheville, it's also an invitation to imagine a church which puts love of neighbor at the heart of its practice. While it's true that the street ministry movement grew out of a response to the spiritual needs of people without homes, maybe it's also true that The Church of the Advocate, and other faith communities like it, are a beacon for the future of the church.

The Rev. Dr. Deborah Little Wyman
Founder and Missioner, common cathedral and Ecclesia Ministries
(Ecclesiaministriesmission.weebly.org)
Author of Church Under the Tree (2000) and Street Stories (2015)

# INTRODUCTION

Red doors on churches have long been a symbol of sanctuary, refuge, and safety. When I first saw the red door of the Church of the Advocate at sidewalk level, leading into the old undercroft of Trinity Episcopal Church in Asheville, North Carolina, I was told that it led to a worshipping community for and by people who were experiencing being unhoused and underserved. My clergy brain started asking silent questions: Who was it that entered this door? What did they find? Was it a holy space? Was it unsafe? What was the worship like? What social services were offered? Was it the social justice poster child of the diocese or parish? Was it a splash in the pan, someone's well-meant initiative that could not, in the end, be sustained. Or was the Spirit of God moving behind that door, filling the hearts and minds of those who showed up; a place of abiding peace and sincere hospitality?

Little did I know that I would become part of the Church of the Advocate as its vicar in the next year. My husband and I had lived apart for a few years so I could complete the commitment I had made to the parish where I was serving and he could make a transition toward retirement. I finally said goodbye to the beloved parish, St. Paul's in Wilmington, North Carolina, and we made our home in Asheville. Hoping for a part-time position in Asheville, I met with Bishop Jose McLaughlin and he assigned me to Church of the Advocate to serve as their vicar.

I had some past experience with providing sacramental and pastoral support to a church like the Advocate, St. Mary's Episcopal Church and Outreach in Jacksonville, Florida. As Bishop Jose described the ministry at the Advocate, I was intrigued. So, in October of 2019, with years of ordained ministry experience in traditional churches, I walked through that red door with a mix of anticipation and trepidation.

Here is a snapshot of what I found when I arrived. On Sunday mornings, when the red door was opened at noon, people who had been waiting outside would amble in. Some would plug their phones into wall outlets. Others would head to tables and chairs that were set up with paper and pens, free books, adult coloring books with colored felt-tip pens and colored pencils. Coffee, juice, water and snacks were available.

Just before 1:30, when the worship service started, individuals would set up three rows of chairs in a horseshoe shape in front of the altar. The altar would be prepared, with grape juice and communion wafers. Bulletins would be ready to hand out. As the musicians would begin to play, people would move into the circle to wait for the service to begin. An average of thirty to forty people would be seated in the circle. There were chairs for those who wished to remain outside the circle. Some would choose to sit on the floor propped up against the wall or curled up in a corner to catch a nap.

Someone in the circle would be asked to light the altar candles; someone else to carry the processional cross; someone else to read the assigned scripture reading; and someone to administer the chalice. The sermon was a short story or life example based on the gospel. The Prayers of the People consisted of simple invitations to name thanksgivings, concerns. The people responded out loud without reserve. They were thankful for the simplest of things and they were honestly raw in naming their concerns and fears. During communion it wasn't unusual to see a person from the streets serving the chalice to a wealthy volunteer. After people received communion they would line up for healing prayers and anointing.

After the service ended, there was a rush of activity as round folding tables were brought out and the partition on the kitchen counter was opened to reveal a hot meal that included mounds of baked chicken or lasagna, bright steamed vegetables, potatoes or rice, salad, hot rolls, lemonade and water. And there was never a Sunday without dessert. Guests were joined at the tables by volunteers or visiting church groups and they would eat casually and chat, lingering until 3:00 when it was time to close up and begin cleaning.

After worship people could also visit Sole Mates, the shoe closet; The Well, a nursing station; and The Basics, supplies for daily living needs.

The combination of worship and meals and other forms of support have had to be adapted through the years in order to accommodate the needs and abilities of those who arrive each Sunday as worshippers, as leaders, and as supporters.

As I worshiped and ministered alongside the dedicated leaders and volunteers, I witnessed both the suffering and the wisdom of those who came to us. I came to appreciate and better comprehend the vital role that a supportive diocese and generous, mission-minded parishes and dedicated individuals play in sustaining a ministry that stands out near the margins, far from the center of the mainstream Church.

While I had always been firmly planted with both feet inside the workings of the churches where I served, I had watched and celebrated the ministries of people who were drawn to the outside fringes of their congregations and of society. Being at the Advocate was for me the missing piece and I felt God was providentially completing the jigsaw puzzle of my ministry. I ended up claiming that this last call before retirement was "the icing on the cake" of my thirty years as a priest. I prayed that I could handle the job and that I would once again experience our imaginative God moving among this community with inspiration and sustenance.

Whenever we experience God's movements among us and attempt to capture and describe them, a holy type of convergence is bound to surface. Individuals, previously unknown to each other, meet. They discover what they have in common. These shared interests, skills or passions start to form a synergism, further enthusing what has become a partnership or a group. And, from what has converged through them, God creates something new and timely and beneficial. Church of the Advocate was born of such a holy convergence. Individuals uniquely gifted for this ministry have continued to respond to the call to serve there.

New endeavors and new ministries are continuously being born. Each one occurs at a given point in time, in a given place, with people who bring unique gifts, passions and drives. When these ministries complete their life cycle, they diminish and come to a close. Some are short-lived. Their sails are filled with the winds of the Spirit, but for a short course. Some are highly successful, and attempts are made to replicate them. Replication may be elusive, because the unique work of the Holy Spirit in a particular place cannot be merely imitated in other places. And, finally, there are those ministries abide through the years and become hallmarks of the Church's identity.

As we came out of the Covid pandemic, I wondered if Church of the Advocate would be sustainable. Would resources dry up? Would new initiatives, begun as a response to the needs of those who were unhoused and unemployed during Covid, render us no longer necessary? Would we need to change course? Or would we come through the shut-down steady and sure?

This book began as a project of gathering narratives from people who, through the years, had been involved with Church of the Advocate. In 2020 when our church buildings were closed during Covid,

I searched through information about Church of the Advocate. Minutes and notes from meetings only covered the most recent years, and I found a folder of old photos and newspaper articles. Wanting to fill in the gaps of a sparse narrative, I contacted former vicars and deacons and leaders who had substantial involvement with the Advocate over its twenty-five-year presence in the Episcopal Diocese of Western North Carolina. Each person was generous with their time, their memories and their insights. Their recollections are a great gift of witness to God's movements in the lives of those who have given and received through this ministry.

Church of the Advocate calls to mind Jesus's parables about the kingdom of God. It is like the pearl of great price, the treasure hidden in a field, a lost sheep, a lost coin. In time, the people and stories of the Advocate could easily be looked over and lost to memory. I felt compelled to search them out and preserve them. This narrative is an endeavor to share a treasure trove of wisdom, healing, and transformation.

Each person whom I interviewed was asked to share their experience at the Advocate, beginning with the chronology and historical context of their time there. Then they were asked to describe their ministry and to share personal stories that were poignant to them. And, finally, they were asked to offer any insights they gained about themselves, the church, and the people they served.

Ellen Weig researched and provided newspaper articles from the Asheville Citizen-Times. These articles, which contributed to the writing of the book, are available in the office of Church of the Advocate. Gerald Ashby went through the many photos he and others have contributed through the years to find images that support the narrative. Gary Whalen formatted the images for the publication of the book and produced the cover image. They have my gratitude for their contributions.

Those who were interviewed have provided a wealth of knowledge which gives the Church a sacred window through which to witness the healing and saving power of God's love as experienced in the presence and ministry of Jesus among those whom he commanded us to serve, "the least of these (Matthew 25:40)." And, the stories tell of how "the least of these" ministered to those of us who are drawn to serve them. The stories contained here are but a gleaning from the many individuals who have served through the years.

Rather than try to blend the interviews into a singular narrative, I have attempted to let the voices of those who were interviewed remain distinct. As their stories are read, I believe they offer us a vantage point that opens our minds, hearts, and our volition to enlarge our capacity to encounter the Church as community formed around Jesus' invitation to new life and directed by the ever-changing choreography of the Holy Spirit.

## A list of those who contributed, and their current positions:

The Rev. Judith Whelchel, Rector of St. James Episcopal Church, Black Mountain, NC; founding vicar of Church of the Advocate

The Rev. Deacon Bill Jamieson, retired, President of the Micah Institute, Asheville, NC; founding deacon at Church of the Advocate

Mary Sorrells, retired teacher, former music leader at Church of the Advocate

The Rev. Deacon Jacque Combs, deacon at Grace Episcopal Church, Fletcher, NC; Social Worker; former music leader, Church of the Advocate

The Rt. Rev. Brian Cole, Bishop of East Tennessee; former vicar of Church of the Advocate

The Rev. Tom Brackett, Manager for Church Planting and Mission Development, The Episcopal Church; former vicar of Church of the Advocate

The Rev. Deacon Peggy Buchanan, retired deacon at Trinity Episcopal Church and Church of the Advocate

The Rev. Vic Mansfield, retired priest, former vicar of Church of the Advocate

Rhonda Candler Kilby, retired nurse, former Director and Board Member at Church of the Advocate

Brother John Huebner, Missioner, Order of St. Francis; former pastor, worship leader and teacher at Church of the Advocate

Dereck Moody, former member of Church of the Advocate

Bill Dockendorf, former leader and Board Member at Church of the Advocate

Gerald Ashby, former Music Coordinator and Webmaster for Church of the Advocate

The Rev. Dena Whalen, retired priest, former Vicar of Church of the Advocate

# THIS IS A CHURCH!

*Judith Whelchel and Bill Jamieson*

In 1997, Judith Whelchel, fresh out of seminary, found herself assigned to Trinity Episcopal Church in Asheville, North Carolina. From within this large, well-established, historic downtown church, she felt a strong desire to get outside its brick walls to serve Christ among those who had no such safety and structure. Bill Jamieson describes her as having been "a gritty, small woman, who was pregnant at the time. She got out on the street and literally started serving people."

Bill, a deacon in the Episcopal Church, was living in Asheville and was volunteering at Hospitality House (now Homeward Bound), which was located in First Presbyterian Church. Just before Christmas, the director of Hospitality House told Bill that the clergyperson who was associated with them couldn't be there for the Christmas Eve service. Bill asked Judith Whelchel if she would take the service.

Bennett Sims, retired bishop of the Diocese of Atlanta, joined Judith and Bill for that service. All three of them were incredibly moved by those who had come to worship. Bill commented, "There's something about the rhythm of our liturgy that gives dignity to people who are not usually afforded dignity." People would come up to the altar with tears in their eyes. As a woman known to Bill and Judith was receiving the cup during communion, she asked if they would baptize her baby. Afterward, Bennett proclaimed, "This is a church!"

Soon afterward, in the new year, when Judith and Bill were called to provide a funeral service for a homeless woman they had come to know, they further realized that a sacramental ministry was coalescing among people who had become a community.

Together, Judith and Bill began to engage in this emerging ministry. They went on foot to locations in downtown Asheville such as Pritchard Park, the bus station, the Hospitality House day center called AHOPE, and the jail. Judith also met with Debbie Little to learn more about the model begun at Boston Common.

After Bill met Debbie Little, when she was a participant on a pilgrimage he led, he and his wife, Kennon, went to see what kind of ministry Debbie was doing in a large city park in Boston. Debbie had started to meet with homeless people at Boston Common in 1994 while having her lunch outside in the park. As she befriended them and heard their stories, she began to perceive a need, perhaps an opportunity, that was beckoning for a response from the Church. As she imagined her part in it, she was motivated to complete studies begun at General Theological Seminary, earn her Master's in Divinity degree, and seek ordination in the Episcopal Church.

Two days after Debbie was ordained, she continued the call that had already begun and "put on a knapsack full of socks, string, a first aid kit, meal and shelter lists, a prayer book, healing oil, AA meeting lists, chapsticks, and peanut butter and jelly sandwiches," all of which she carried to Boston Common. The first worship service of Holy Eucharist in Boston Common was held on Easter Sunday in 1996 (www.commoncathedral.org).

What Bill found when he went to observe the ministry at Boston Common, was the most authentic church he had ever seen. While attending the Sunday worship at Boston Common he noticed two men who were sitting off to the side, observing the worship service in the park. They told Bill, "We're Jewish, living in a facility for retired Jews. But we come here every Sunday because of the powerful experience of the Holy."

Drawing from that model and having met with Bishop Bob Johnson (then bishop of the Diocese of Western North Carolina) Judith and Bill began going to Pritchard Park every Thursday with peanut butter sandwiches, coffee, and communion. After she and Bill did this a few times, Judith decided to approach Bob Johnson with the idea of establishing a congregation without walls, modeled after the one in Boston Common. In the meantime, Bill contacted the local newspaper. After an article featuring a large color photo showing Judith holding up the consecrated bread in the park, Bishop Johnson caught the vision and a new ministry was begun in the Diocese of Western North Carolina.

Judith and Bill continued taking a card table to Pritchard Park to offer Holy Eucharist and sandwiches to anyone who showed up. Those who had musical instruments began to play for the service and a jam session evolved. They did this for about a year.

As Bill reflected on Judith's early ministry, he said, "Judith did extraordinary things. She had to fight people's misperceptions of what she wanted to do." When she and Bill decided to offer ministry to the homeless who were arrested and in the county jail, Judith faced several obstacles before she could get the credentials to visit inside the jail. She would go and sit at bus stops with people in order to meet them. She saw the need for a foot ministry and so she arranged for Bill and herself to wash the dirty feet of people who were living outdoors, and then, a nurse who worked in podiatry followed up with treatment.

Bill remembers that as he was washing the feet of one young woman, she began to cry. When he asked if he was hurting her, she said, "No. This is the first time I've been touched gently by a man."

Though the Common Cathedral (as it came to be known) on Boston Common was intentionally a church without walls, Judith saw the need to provide an indoor space in which people could get respite from the weather and the distractions of the streets. This move was also necessitated by the fact that Judith had to get a permit every single time they wanted to meet in Pritchard Park. Judith had procured a van and was allowed to park it at All Souls Cathedral. Several members at All Souls began to support the ministry. Judith knew that the old undercroft at Trinity was not being used. It was in disrepair, with the plaster falling off the walls, and she recalled the stench of mold and the leavings of church mice. When she won willingness from the diocese and from Trinity to let her use the space, people from All Souls, including Gary Kovak, got it cleaned up and painted. After her Sunday morning duties, Judith would go to Trinity's undercroft in the afternoon where she swung wide the red door which opened right onto the Church Street sidewalk. Once they moved inside for worship and meals, the street name quickly became the Red Door. If you ask some people in Asheville today where the Church of the Advocate is, they may hesitate. If you ask them where the Red Door is, they immediately tell you to "walk down Church Street and you'll see it."

The location in the undercroft made it possible to organize hot meals instead of sandwiches. Judith recruited about twelve Episcopal churches to bring food on Sundays. The worship service began at 1:30 with the meal following. This was so that people could attend their own churches before bringing food to the Advocate. When members of a church arrived with the food on Sundays they were invited to participate with the gathered community around both the communion table and the meal tables. Those who were unhoused served the meal. Both housed and unhoused were welcomed and served by the homeless.

In 1999 and 2000 the soup kitchens/agencies that are now active in downtown Asheville did not exist. People were hungry. The numbers coming to the Red Door for a meal got up to 175 people. Because this number of people far exceeded the capacity of the space, this caused many of them to remain outside. Because of the crowded conditions, both communion and the meals were taken to those who remained outside and police had to be called to come and maintain order. As the large number of people crowding into the undercroft and out on the sidewalk continued to cause problems, Judith talked with the police chief and it was determined that it was unsafe for so many to gather in that space. The kitchen was closed for a month. The numbers decreased to the fifty who regularly came to worship together, and they brought their own food to share.

As time went on, the style and content of the Sunday worship services took on a shape of their own. Bishop Johnson directed that the eucharistic prayers of the Book of Common Prayer be used. Judith adapted to the context by simplifying and shortening the worship service. She found that an oral service with no books or paper bulletins worked best. The readings consisted of the Gospel and one lesson. Her sermons were brief, and she invited dialogue with those gathered. The music was familiar and singable.

How did the name *Church of the Advocate* come to be? Bill recalls that from the beginning they got the name "Advocate" from the name given by Christ for the Holy Spirit as found in the Gospel according to John (14:16): "And I will ask the Father, and he will give you another Advocate, to be with you forever." The name also appealed to Judith because the Church of the Advocate in Philadelphia was where the first ordination of women in the Episcopal Church took place in 1974.

Judith and Bill approached the diocese to receive Church of the Advocate as a parish. They were told that three things determine parish status: a stable community of members, who have a building, and are able to financially support a priest. Since Church of the

Advocate was not financially self-sustaining and did not have its own property, the diocese defined it as a "Worshipping Community."

The inception of this worshipping community was born of Judith and Bill's deep desire to get outside the walls of the buildings and institutional structures of the traditional church. They sought a way to seek and serve Christ "in the least of these." And while it has from the beginning and always will be financially dependent on the support of the traditional Church, the unique charism, the spiritual gift, of this community was born of Judith's and Bill's deep sense of call.

From among those who were regular members of the worship circle on Sundays, Judith formed a group to make leadership decisions about Church of the Advocate. As part of the requirements to be recognized as a Worshipping Community, they had to come before the Annual Convention of the Diocese of Western North Carolina with a mission statement. When the group met to create the mission statement, E. Perry Coe Jr., who is still a regular presence, said the mission was simply to "Love the Lord your God with all your heart, with all your soul, with all your mind and with all your strength; and love your neighbor as yourself." (Mark 12:30) This became the first mission statement of the Church of the Advocate.

The first year they sought to be approved by the Diocese as a Worshipping Community, they did not get enough votes. Judith worked through the following year to explain the ministry and gain the support of the clergy. The next year they won the vote. Finally, at the next Diocesan Annual Convention, they were approved and welcomed as a Worshipping Community into the diocese. Perry was the first lay delegate to represent Church of the Advocate at the Annual Convention.

Bill remembers when his daughter chose to have his granddaughter baptized at the Advocate. The gospel that day was about Mary Magdalene. When someone remarked that Mary Magdalene was a prostitute, a woman in the congregation said, "What's wrong with that? That's how I fed my kids."

When the Columbine shooting happened in April of 1999, those at the Advocate talked about boycotting Walmart because the shooters had bought their ammunition there. One member said, "I have some violence in myself to work out first before I go out and try to figure out violence in other people."

Judith served in this ministry for five years. She went on to work for the ServantLeader Institute, leading retreats and pilgrimages, and became a spiritual director. Upon her departure she encouraged the development of a board/vestry. She currently serves as the rector of St. James Episcopal Church in Black Mountain, North Carolina. Bill Jamieson is retired and lives with his wife Kennan in Asheville.

*Judith at Pritchard Park*

*Judith and Bill, undercroft, Trinity*

*Gary Kovach, Judith, Bill*

*Judith and Bishop Bob Johnson in prayer group*

# LONGING TO BELONG

*Jacque Combs*

There came to be a core of people from the Cathedral of All Souls who joined together in ministry at the Advocate when it moved into the undercroft of Trinity Church. They all shared the same values and vision as they gave substance to the community forming at the Advocate. Those from All Souls included Judith Whelchel, Bill Jamieson, Jacque Combs, Mary Sorrells, and Carroll Ensley. Jacque, Mary and Carroll all sang in the cathedral choir and went to the Advocate as music leaders.

Although Jacque was later ordained a deacon, she was a layperson the entire time she served at the Advocate. A very useful convergence occurred when Jacque began to give her time and talent as a musician to the Advocate. It happened that her career was in mental health and substance abuse. She had specialized in The Clubhouse Model used by Fountain House, a national mental health nonprofit fighting to improve health, increase opportunity, and end social and economic isolation for people most impacted by mental illness. (Fountainhouse.org)

Jacque was using this model in her work with individuals who were formerly in psychiatric institutions and had been resettled back into communities. The whole premise of this model of psycho-social rehabilitation is belonging, relationships, and having a voice. As the social worker in the group, Jacque had an astute understanding of the needs and gifts of the people who came to the Advocate. She also was the one particularly equipped to intervene when someone was being disruptive.

Judith had a specific motivation for asking Jacque to help with music. Judith wanted her to provide a musical setting for a Eucharistic Prayer that Judith had written. Each Sunday, Jacque recalls, "As the circle for worship-in-the-round formed we felt the presence of the Holy Spirit as a diversity of individuals coalesced into a communion of trust. Also palpable in the circle was the invitation to be vulnerable and present to one another."

Jacque remembers that the Advocate was a both/and place. The old and the new, tradition and exploration, were blended. There were baptisms and weddings and funerals, all carefully crafted to give sacramental and pastoral meaning for those involved. Judith and the musicians followed the traditional seasons of the Church year and held to the traditional framework for eucharistic worship as set forth in the Book of Common Prayer. However, they were agile in allowing the framework to be adapted so as to be relevant and to have an authentic, indigenous expression.

Flexibility has long been a strength of the prayer book as it is employed for worshipping communities across many cultures and abilities. In the worship circle on any given Sunday there may be someone caught in the vicious trap of addiction who can't manage a treatment plan; mental illness that goes unchecked because the person can't manage a stable drug regimen; someone who is trying to come through after racial violence, rape, abuse, theft; those with medical conditions such as diabetes, cancer, multiple sclerosis; those in chronic pain because of an injury, a bad tooth, a foot sore; those who lack good vision and hearing. The list could go on.

"An Order for Celebrating the Holy Eucharist" in the prayer book provides guidelines that give shape to the weekly liturgy. The guidelines include an invitation to "Gather in the Lord's Name" through a welcome and music. They would "Proclaim and Respond to the Word of God", which would always include a gospel reading, a teaching, dialogue, and music. They would "Pray for the World and the Church" giving voice to the issues that people in the circle faced each week. They were also mindful to name leaders in social justice (such as Martin Luther King, Jr. and Sojourner Truth) as well as the usual civic leaders included in the Prayers of the People. They would "Exchange the Peace" and "Prepare the Table", "Make Eucharist", "Break the Bread", and "Share the Gifts of God."

After the altar table was prepared, Jacque would lead the circle in singing *Dear Father,* which she composed and is on the CD they produced:

> Dear Father, hear my voice in the wilderness crying
> Crying for some faith, for some hope, some love,
> Father for your love
> Dry my tears with your laughter
> Call my years with your ever after
> Father, hear my voice in the wilderness crying
> Dear Father, hear my voice.

As Jacque continued to play background music on guitar, Judith would pray The Great Thanksgiving in the form of the "Story of Salvation" in these words:

> So the story goes that at the beginning of
> God's creating there was vast darkness
> And God brought forth light
> placing it in the heavens
> God separated the waters from the lands
> God caused life to grow, plants and seeds and fruits
> God brought forth living beings, crawling ones,
> swimming ones, the winged fowl and wildlife
> Each in their own kind

And then God chose to put God's
own face on creation
And God created woman and
man in God's own image
And then God looked on all that God
had created and God said it is good
And God blessed creation

From the beginning we were created
good and blessed by our God
And then God set creation free
Blessed and good, we were sent forth to
live and move and have our being

Sometimes in our freedom we were
able to live in our wholeness
We were able to love ourselves,
to love our sisters and our brothers,
And to love our God
But sometimes events arise in life
And we find we cannot practice love of self
And we are not loving towards
our sisters and our brothers
And we feel far from God
But the good news is that it is God's nature always
to call us back to who we were created to be
And God has done that work throughout history

The Bible tells us of God calling the people Israel
out of bondage and slavery
Into a promised land
Kings and judges came forth to restore
justice and to be a light to the nations
The prophets rose up calling an
oppressed people in bondage

To remember who they were created to be
To ground themselves in that, and to live

And Jesus came and walked among us
Calling all to be in love with
themselves, one another and God
He called forth the abandoned and forgotten
ones, the orphans, the widows, the poor
And he called forth the despised ones,
the tax collectors, prostitutes, lepers
He called forth the sick ones, the
blind, the deaf and the lame
And he spoke with them and ate
with them and touched them
He loved them into their wholeness

God's work of love continued in history
We remember the saints through the ages
Who called us to love
And we remember the saints in our day and life
Who call us to love

Jesus came and called people
Out of a world bent on domination and oppression
Into a world of love
People listened to Jesus and they followed him
In a world that preached power Jesus preached love
He became a threat to the state and was
crucified as a political criminal
At a place called Calvary
For three days it seemed that the power of
death was stronger than the spirit of life
That oppression had the final voice over love
But we know how the story ends

And we know that after three days
Jesus rose from the dead
And we know that the Spirit of love is
stronger than the power of death

On the night before Jesus died he
invited his friends around his table
And he took the bread and he took
the cup and he blessed them
And then he blessed his friends
And asked them to share the bread and the cup
Remembering that they share his spirit of love
The Christ's body is broken but it is made
whole as we practice love. Alleluia.

The prayer of thanksgiving, the telling of the story of salvation would end with a reprise of the song:

For some faith, for some hope, some love, Father, for your love.

Dear Father, hear our voice in
the wilderness crying,
Dear Father.

Jacque recalled that from week to week, and even from moment to moment during worship, they were never able to predict what would happen next. However, in the midst of all the chaos and the ever-changing social terrain made up of those who showed up on any given Sunday, it was always a sacramental space that held the mystic presence of God. Jacque reflected, "When someone comes in who can hardly walk or stay awake, enduring the sheer exhaustion of living on the street, how do we meet them where they are, receive what they bring, and have the presence to offer them what God would have us give them? There was a very deep wisdom from the circle."

As Jacque sees it, the only way for the Advocate to be true to its call was be a welcome place for the whole of the human condition. It was a messy place where a lot of vulnerable people were showing up. The core group and those who were regulars in the circle were able to create a place where they could hold all the messiness, all the human conditions, and talk about it. In that they expected people to show up broken, there wasn't judgment about brokenness even when it surfaced in the leaders and volunteers.

To Jacque, the circle was a place of deep longing. It offered a safe space to gather and hold a collective longing in those present. Out of that longing comes a sense of belonging. "The space allowed us to be broken open so we could experience being who we are and where we are. It held the tension of who we most want to be and who we no longer want to be. Therein lies the grace."

Each worship service ended with The Micah Song, based on Micah 6:8 and set to music by Jacque.

> God has taught us my friends what is good
> What has the Lord required of us
> But to do justice, love kindness and
> to walk humbly with our God
> Walk ever so humbly with our God.

There was always the necessity to be evaluating what was happening. Every Sunday they were holding a similar space, but not exactly the same. There was a stable core group of worshippers but dynamics were always changing. After a while the circle and the style of worship they had planted began to shift. While worship was going on inside, two to three hundred started coming to the Red Door waiting to be fed. As the worship space got crowded the leaders had to establish new parameters.

Jacque expressed the challenge in words something like this, "When you plant a mission you want to have some control over what's happening. How do we *be* Jesus? How do we have this welcoming table open to all? How can we be agile in adapting while we steadfastly respect the dignity of every human being, respond to the needs they bring to us, and all the while keep boundaries that provide a sense of safety and order? To hold a space, you have to define the expectations in that space. And yet the challenge, presented by the burdens and sheer numbers of the unhoused, unstable and under-served who came each week, defied any sustainable expectations."

Jacque attributes Judith's vision and then Brian Cole's carrying it forward as the glue that held the whole endeavor together. When Brian's ministry as Vicar of the Advocate ended, it was also time for Jacque to move on.

*Jacque (center) with friends on a Sunday*

# LOVING CHAOS

*Mary Sorrells*

Mary Sorrells was among the group from the Cathedral of All Souls who responded to Judith's appeal in 2001 for music leaders. Mary began to play guitar and lead the worship music at Advocate on Sundays. A teacher by profession, she moved into the context with a natural instinct for using music to welcome people and relate to them. She provided worship music at Advocate for ten years.

From day one Mary would ask people as they came in, "Do you have a song you would like to sing?" One Sunday she asked this question as a man came through the door. In response, he came in and sat right down at the piano and started to play. They learned that Spencer Taylor was his name and that he was a Muslim. He can be heard singing "Lean On Me" on the CD and is the one who had to be brought out of prison for the recording sessions.

How did Advocate become holy ground for Mary? She remembers being struck by the absence of "masks" in this unorthodox church. "Nobody wore the "masks" we get accustomed to wearing. People were honest about what they thought, no matter how blunt it might come across. There were no pretenses. What you saw was what you got."

One Sunday the gospel was about Jesus calling Matthew the tax collector:

<sup>9</sup>As Jesus was walking along, he saw a man called Matthew sitting at the tax booth; and he said to him, "Follow me." And he got up and followed him. <sup>10</sup>And as he sat at dinner in the house, many tax collectors and sinners came and were sitting with him and his disciples. <sup>11</sup>When the Pharisees saw this, they said to his disciples, "Why does your teacher eat with tax collectors and sinners?" <sup>12</sup>But when he heard this, he said, "Those who are well have no need of a physician, but those who are sick.<sup>13</sup>Go and learn what this means, 'I desire mercy, not sacrifice.' For I have come to call not the righteous but sinners." <sup>14</sup>Then the disciples of John came to him, saying, "Why do we and the Pharisees fast often, but your disciples do not fast?" <sup>15</sup>And Jesus said to them, "The wedding guests cannot mourn as long as the bridegroom is with them, can they? The days will come when the bridegroom is taken away from them, and then they will fast. <sup>16</sup>No one sews a piece of unshrunk cloth on an old cloak, for the patch pulls away from the cloak, and a worse tear is made. <sup>17</sup>Neither is new wine put into old wineskins; otherwise, the skins burst, and the wine is spilled, and the skins are destroyed; but new wine is put into fresh wineskins, and so both are preserved." (Matthew 9:9-17)

Judith told them that the tax collector stepped out of his collection box and out of the box of his life and she asked those in the circle to ponder some questions: "When have you stepped out of your box? Have you ever been invited to step out of your box? Is there anyone in your life that you need to allow to step out of their box?"

At that time in Mary's life, her father had dementia. The day before that Sunday's service, he had become quite disoriented while in her small home. Mary responded to Judith's questions by saying that she needed to let her father step out of the box she had always known him to be in so that she could be present to him in his current condition. Spencer came over to Mary, kissed her on her cheek gave her a hug and said, "Your father is going to be alright." She started to cry and he held her. He ministered to her. And Mary discovered that, whereas she would not have done so at her church, at the Church of the Advocate she had let her own mask down and was met with tender love and assurance.

Mary is grateful that she learned to be present with those who seemed so different from her. She became more aware of obstacles that arose because of the differences. She had on a wool blazer one day and one of the women told her, "Anyone wearing what you're wearing does not know what it is like to be me."

Before Mary came to Church of the Advocate, homeless people were off her radar. In this community she learned their names and they learned hers. Being known by name was for Mary a profound part of being in community.

Another insight for Mary came from E. Perry Coe, Jr. One day he shared a saying in the circle: "When one door closes, others are standing open." She had always heard it this way: "When one door closes another one opens." We tend to stand staring at the closed door, waiting for another to open. From Perry's version Mary saw it a new way. When one door closes there are several opportunities already open and waiting to be explored.

Because Mary's guitar was so integral to her music and her ministry, her heart ached at the thought that if she were homeless, she wouldn't have a guitar. So, she would go around after the worship offering her guitar to people who could play. One Sunday, she came back into the main room after meeting with a women's group that took place during the meal. Her guitar was gone. The homeless people were very upset that someone had walked out with her guitar and case.

Yet, everybody there told her that since it had surely been sold by now, there was no use in even looking for it.

That evening she was at an event and Gary Kovach asked her how she felt when she learned they found her guitar. She didn't even know it had been found! He told her that two of the men had gone out looking for it and saw a man sitting on the case, smoking a cigarette. They said to him, "Are you going to take the guitar back or are we?"

During the time that the production of the CD was in the works, Jacque Combs, her wife Kim, and Mary were staying overnight at Room in the Inn, an emergency nighttime shelter for women, hosted by various churches. They asked the women who were staying there as guests, "Do you have a song to share?" One woman, Leonora Boyd, sang a song called "Stumblin' Block." A month later, when it was time to record, they wanted to find Leonora to record her song on the CD. Mary, a teacher, was at school looking at her paperwork and saw that Leonora Boyd was the mother of one of her students. The grandmother was taking care of the child.

Mary asked the grandmother if her daughter sang the song, to which the grandmother replied, "I taught her that song!" She told Mary which street corner Leonora frequented. Mary found her and got her involved in the recording sessions. Leonora's song is on the CD; her photo on the insert. In addition to the good fortune of finding Leonora, Mary recalls that when the next parent conference occurred the grandmother, mother, and daughter all showed up. Because of this encounter with Mary, they were now more at ease with the school. And, Leonora can be heard on the CD singing *Stumblin' Block* and *Holding On,* sung a cappella with loose meter:

**I'm Still Holding On** by Luther Barnes
They said I wouldn't make it
They said I wouldn't be here today
They said I'd never amount to anything
But I'm glad to say, that I'm on my way
And I'm going more and more each day
There were many that started out with me
But now, they've gone astray
But I'm still holding on to his hand.

"Loving chaos" is a description of the Advocate that resonates with Mary. We discover Love moving in the midst of chaos which enables us, in turn, to learn to love the chaos because we have learned to expect God to show up precisely in the chaos.

Mary still runs into some of the people with whom she worshipped. They hug and greet each other. They still know each other by name.

*Mary Sorrells — far right*

# HOLDING THE SPACE

*Brian Cole*

.

Brian Cole was in the process to become a priest in the Episcopal Church when he began an internship with Judith at the Advocate in 1999. When the time came for Judith to leave, Brian became the lay vicar of the Advocate, with Bill Jamieson remaining as Deacon for a time. When Brian was ordained in 2002 he became the vicar.

After his ordination, Brian was called to a part-time position on the clergy staff at the Cathedral of All Souls while he continued to serve as vicar on Sunday afternoons at the Advocate. Part of his role was to foster good relations between the Advocate and All Souls, which was the primary supporting church at that time. When Brian was called to serve full time at All Souls, he moved on from the Advocate. Deacon Anne Fritschner, who was devoted to the ministry of the Advocate, stepped up to the helm and kept things going.

Brian shared some powerful stories about his time at Church of the Advocate.

Because music on Sundays continued to be an incredible convergence of diverse and talented musicians, Judith had begun the groundwork to get a CD produced and worked with a local radio station to set up a recording session, featuring the talents of these musicians. St. James Episcopal Church in Hendersonville awarded them a grant to fund the CD. Brian carried on with this initiative until the project was completed in 2002. Brian pointed out that this project accomplished a couple of things. First, it showed that a person can be both homeless and incredibly talented. And, because all sales were 100% profit on the two thousand copies made, all the proceeds went to the people who performed on the CD and in support of Hospitality House.

Just as the Advocate is a place of convergence where the housed and the unhoused, the haves and the have-nots, meet, it has also served as a threshold for passersby to meet Christ in "the other." During Brian's time at the Advocate, Kenneth Leach, an English Anglican priest, author, and Christian activist came to preach at the Cathedral of All Souls. Brian invited him to come to the worship service at the Advocate and Leach led in the reflection. They gave him copy of the CD and he did a review of it.

Another memory stems from a serendipitous convergence on the sidewalk outside the Red Door. Brian continued the practice he inherited from Judith of worshipping in a circle. An average of fifty people were coming inside on Sundays, about half of whom were actively engaged in the worship circle. In addition, there was a multitude of people outside waiting for the meal. After the worship ended Brian would open the door to see if any of the people outside wanted communion. For him it was a tangible experience of throwing open the doors of the larger Church and going forth into the world.

One Sunday afternoon a priest from Boston, in town to do a wedding, was taking a walk in downtown Asheville before catching his flight home. He happened to be walking up the sidewalk along Church Street as the red door opened up and out came Brian with communion. Moved to tears, he followed Brian inside and they had a conversation.

Twice a week, Brian went to AHOPE, a day center which is a program of Homeward Bound of Western North Carolina. He saw the need for a counselor/social worker to be available on location at

AHOPE rather than the people having to make their way to other locations to get these services. Because of this, the Church of the Advocate funded a licensed counselor/social worker to be located at AHOPE .

At one point they were feeding up to two hundred people each Sunday. One man, who suffered from schizophrenia, got agitated and pulled a knife on Brian. It was the homeless members that day who called for a pause in the Sunday meals in order to protect the circle.

E. Perry Coe, Jr., who has been involved at Advocate since the beginning, is part of Brian's story. On the first day of worship without a meal, Perry brought a bunch of apples. They sliced up the apples and ate together. The homeless brought food to share for a while. Later, churches were invited to resume their involvement.

Perry, who is nearing his eightieth year, is a disabled veteran. He was a medic in Vietnam. It was the war that broke him, he says. Although he currently lives in a house, he has had periods of homelessness through the years and has a long history with, and great knowledge of, the services offered by churches in the area over the past few decades. He remembers meeting Judith Whelchel and Bill Jamieson in Pritchard Park as they offered a worship service and peanut butter sandwiches. He remembers the foot washing ministry.

Brian recalls Perry as being like St. Francis. "He would walk around with a backpack, pull out a book and give it to you. It was uncanny how relevant each book was to the person who received it." In fact, Perry became a Secular Franciscan and a Domestic Member of the Brothers and Sisters of Charity. This is someone who associates with the monastic order while living and serving in the context of a secular life. Perry is still giving books to people when he can tell they have a desire and are open to receiving one. As well as being the first delegate from Advocate to the Diocesan Annual Convention, Perry was present as one of Brian's sponsors when Brian was ordained a priest.

Brian says that the charism evident at the Advocate through the years is steadfastness. "Our job is to worship and the primary thing was for people to have a safe place that offered worship and provided dignity to everyone who showed up. There was always wisdom in the room. On any given Sunday, there were homeless, college students, and the wealthy who experienced the Sunday gatherings as "real church." There was no sense of us and them. We were all together the Church." Brian witnessed new start-up ministries in Asheville for the unhoused. People from Advocate would be attracted to something new. But after a time, such ministries would end and people would return to the Red Door.

Brian reflected on his feelings of being ill-equipped for this ministry when he ventured outside the Red Door. "What do you do, what do you say, once you arrive at the jail or the bus terminal? What might happen if you invite dialogue during the sermon? There is a risk in not knowing where things will go. How do you pivot and move with the Holy Spirit when you don't know where unfamiliar encounters and open dialogue will take you?"

When Brian first arrived at the Advocate, he thought he was there "to build a community, to gather this motley crew, this merry band and keep them in community." However, he learned that his job was to make a container for each day; to hold a space for God and individuals to meet. His epiphany was that this ministry "is about NOW. There is a certain amount of improvisation that must happen because the only way you can perceive the needs of people and receive the gifts they have to offer is to be present in each moment."

Brian learned a lot about managing different communities at the same time. There was ministry out in the community and on the streets, as well as fulfilling the role of priest in the traditional church setting. There was the art of relating to people, whether appealing to the well-endowed while fund-raising or interacting with individuals while visiting at the jail. Brian reflected, "When you must be constantly adjusting to a variety of situations, pivoting on the move, you find you can only serve authentically when you are anchored in Christ."

Included in author and Episcopal priest Garrett Keizer's book *Help: The Original Human Dilemma,* are insights from an interview he had with Brian. The book is an exploration of the intrinsic human need to give and receive help.

> I spoke not long ago with the Reverend Brian Cole, a young clergyman who works with a congregation of the homeless at the Church of the Advocate in Asheville, North Carolina. With reference to his parishioners in general and to the disabled veterans among them in particular, he said, "We are a society that goes through people." In other words, we are a society that can behave like the robbers [in the parable of the Good Samaritan who beat the man on the side of the road and took all he had].

> Jesus (or Luke) is careful to let us know that all of those who pass by the man on the road see him; the verb saw is repeated every time a new person comes upon the scene. But the Samaritan is the only one who looks—we read that he "drew near"—and the reason is that in addition to seeing a wounded man, he is able to see the possibility that the man might still be alive. In the Samaritan's eyes, the universe is not a closed or predetermined system.

> Brian Cole, the young priest who told me about the society that "goes through people," had this to say about the role of imagination in trying to help them: Most of the people we encounter [that is, street people] want to see their lives transformed. It's often amazing

to sit with them as they experience their pain—but if you just stay there that becomes abusive, and you wind up mining them for sermon illustrations or for some insight about yourself. I need to be able to say, "I can imagine this person not being homeless, I can dream of this person not being addicted, and maybe some of that happening will involve some resources or gifts I bring to this."

Keizer includes Brian Cole's description of a deacon, Gary Kozak who was assigned to St. Mary's Episcopal Church, and was present at AHOPE and at the Church of the Advocate:

Brian is a tall, well-spoken young clergyman. His deacon is a gray-bearded, chain-smoking Vietnam vet, about five-feet-four, a "sort of fireplug" who rolls his eyes whenever he believes Brian "has been played again." Gary is solid, honest, frank, in some ways profane but also a very devout Christian who does the truly hard work every day of working in the shelter.... He's the bouncer if there's a fight. He's also the unofficial counselor, not in a let-me-hold-your-hand way, more in a let-me-kick-your-ass way.... I think if someone came in initially and spent time with Gary, they'd say he's cynical. What I've discovered is that Gary's not cynical. He's deeply committed to basic justice.... He's able to live with the failings and shortcomings of the people he works with because he also has to live in the church, where as people we have higher expectations that often fail us in the very same ways. He's much more likely to bust the chops of the priest or bishop who's shortchanging the gospel than he is to be anything less than compassionate in a way that is calling that homeless person into wholeness.

There is the constant conundrum of discerning whether help is simply giving someone what they want in the moment as opposed to something more. Brian is quoted in the book:

> If the person wants three dollars, give him the three dollars! It was Gary who first told me that two dollars was the cost of Brass Monkey or Night Train. Sure, you can give them two dollars and help them get liquored up, or you can get more deeply involved in their lives. Gary is constantly reminding me to ask the harder question, or to listen harder to the person, and not just get caught up in the initial story that makes them feel good or me feel good.

> When I asked Brian Cole what he did to keep the sadness of his ministry from getting the better of him, he told me of an antique store in Asheville where he sometimes goes on his lunch hour. "People make beautiful things. They make beautiful rugs, beautiful pieces of furniture. I need to remember that not everything is broken, not everything is destroyed, not everything is lost—that some folks made things that worked and lasted and held together."

*Brian Cole at altar*

*Brian Cole and Nicky Merritt*

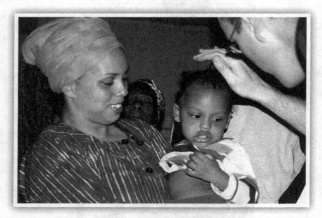

*Bob and Lucia White's child being baptized by Brian*

*Early photo of Perry with Madeleine Plaumbaum*

## Peace of the Road CD

*Peace of the Road CD cover*

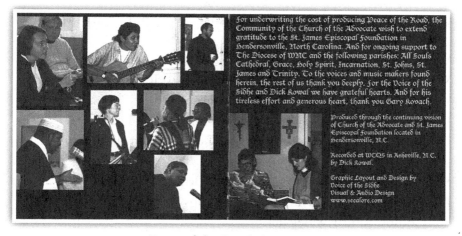

*Peace of the Road CD insert*

Produced by John Gernandt, Voice of the Sidh

The artwork on the cover is John's painting. His wife, Yssabel, and he did all of the graphics. They were very active at the Advocate in those days.

## Contents

Amazing Grace – (John Newton) Bobby Sax, Jacque Combs

Holding On – (Unknown) Leonora Boyd

Micah 6:8 – (Jacque Combs) Jacque Combs, Carroll Ensley Mary Sorrells

Lean on Me – (Bill Withers) Spencer Taylor with: Jacque Combs, Ken Moore, Vanessa Parks, Marlene Gray, Judith Whelchel, Carroll Ensley, Mary Sorrells, Abdul Allam

Good King Wenceslas – (Traditional) John Gernandt & Aaron Thompson

Mi Amigo Jesus – (Jones & Denise Craig) Nicky Merritt, Mary Sorrells

The Cherry Tree Carol – (Traditional) Carroll Ensley

Improvisation – Peter Salvucci

Stand by Me (Unknown) Vanessa Parks

Create in Me (John Michael Talbot) Jacque Combs, Carroll Ensley, Mary Sorrells

Verdigorn's Last Stand – Carol Tibbitts

We will Drive Dull Care Away (Traditional) John Gernandt, Vicki Baker, Cayce Burch, Aaron Thompson

Pescador de Hombres – (Placencia Nora) Nicky Merritt

Gift of Love (Hal Hopson) Jacque Combs, Carroll Ensley, Mary Sorrells

Stumbling Block (unknown) Leonora Boyd

Dear Father/Love Prayer (Jacque Combs, Judith Whelchel) Jacque Combs, Judith Whelchel

Jesus Loves Me (Anna Warner, William Bradbury) Bobby Sax

Let There be Peace on Earth and Let it Begin with Me (Sy Miller, Jill Jackson) Jacque Combs, Sophie Whelchel

# WILL YOU GIVE ME COMMUNION?

*Tom Brackett*

When the Rev. Tom Brackett came to Asheville in 2004, Church of the Advocate did not have a vicar. Tom was soon asked to be on the clergy rota for celebrating and preaching on Sundays. In a short time, Tom's responsibilities and commitment at Advocate increased. One Sunday a month became twice a month and Tom took on the work of coordinating clergy. He also resumed the practice of having congregations come in with food on Sundays and share in the tables of worship and meal. Finally, Tom was asked to serve as vicar of the Church of the Advocate in 2007.

It happens that Tom had done field placement with Debbie Little at *common cathedral* (the outdoor church and street ministry that grew out of the ministry at Boston Common), so he knew about both the relationships and the boundaries that need to be maintained in shared ministry. Tom noted that Judith, Brian, and Anne Fritchner were lovely examples of offering the ministry while keeping healthy boundaries between Trinity, the Diocese and those served by Advocate.

There have been many experiments on how to welcome all who come to the Red Door and, at the same time and in the same space, maintain peace and a worship-friendly environment. Tom recalls that the numbers of people coming into the Red Door on Sundays for food only was uncontrollably disrupting those wanting to worship in the sacred space of the circle. The building space inside could not accommodate both. Tom decided to close the door at the start of the service. If someone got there late, they would be helped to find a seat. Only those in the worship service could share the meal that followed. Once this change was made, someone came up to Tom and said, "Why don't we combine the meal with worship and call the whole thing communion?" What if communion were in the midst of the meal? They tried this, but found that folding the eucharist into the communal meal wasn't feasible because it necessarily diminished the centrality of the worship circle.

Following the pattern of those who preceded him, Tom set aside Thursdays to get out in the community. He led a Thursday prayer service with healing upstairs at AHOPE. He first would serve coffee and help people to their lockers. After the prayer service he would walk the streets with socks, water, and prayers. Folks from the Advocate began to walk with him. By 5 p.m. they would finish the day at Pritchard Park at the center of downtown. Because of this weekly routine, Tom developed a relationship with the Pritchard Park Rangers, who would fill him in on special needs and helpful information about people.

When asked by Bishop Keith Sloan to be the keynote speaker at the 2016 Diocesan Convention in the Diocese of Alabama, Tom included a story of events that took place during his time at the Advocate.

Tom began by bringing attention to God calling Jesus "beloved" at his baptism, and then later, on the Mount of Transfiguration before his descent into Jerusalem. Tom reminded his listeners that, for his baptism, Jesus chose to seek God in the muddy river Jordan rather than take part in the baptismal cleansing in the clean temple pools. Jesus chose to seek his belovedness in the common community experience.

"Belovedness tells us there is nothing we can do to get God to love us more - or to love us less. The world is hungry for belovedness. The world comes to the Church in search of belovedness, and we give them, instead, a sense of importance. Peter confused belovedness for importance in his experience during Jesus's transfiguration."

Tom posed the question: Is it the institutional church, the mystical church, the local congregation? Which church are we describing when we say that belovedness is what we have to offer?

The following is a paraphrased summary of Tom's story, a story of the belovedness he witnessed through the Advocate. In no way does it adequately convey his wonderful style of storytelling.

Tom heard there was a new tienda, a Mexican grocery store, in Asheville. In search of green corn tortillas to use in a recipe, Tom went there and asked the man tending the store, Eduardo, "Do you have any green corn tortillas?" In the course of their conversation Eduardo learned that Tom was an Episcopal priest. He told Tom that a bunch of his friends got together at the parking lot behind an empty Ingle's grocery store and invited Tom to come with him to meet his friends on Fridays after work. The next Friday night Tom showed up, got in Eduardo's truck, and they drove to the out-of-sight parking lot behind the store.

There was every kind of racing car. As the guys were talking about work, family, girls, Eduardo introduced Tom to each man. Tom was the only Anglo guy among these men who were mostly from Juarez, Mexico.

The second time Tom joined them, he noticed a short stocky guy named Angelo. Angelo was the leader of this gang. He asked Tom why he was there. Tom responded by telling him how he met Eduardo at the tienda while looking for green tortillas. Angelo pressed the question, "No, why are you here?" Angelo wondered if Tom was connected to the police.

After being with them for a while, Tom realized what a great group of men this was.

Tom asked them for songs that made them feel close to God. They began to give him CDs of their favorite songs. Angelo came to Tom with a CD of his collection of sacred music, and to protect his image, Angelo asked Tom to keep it secret. Driving home, Tom put it in his CD player and cried his way home as he listened to everything from Ave Maria to Mexican rap songs.

One Friday Angelo asked Tom, "Do your ever have coffee with people?" Angelo was a foreman at a factory, and they agreed to meet on Thursday at 2 p.m. after work. When they met, Angelo told Tom he wanted to tell Tom his story, "me like I am." He told Tom that ever since he was a teenager the monsignor at his church wouldn't let him or his best friend have communion. The monsignor called these two life-long friends wicked. Angelo asked Tom, "If we come to your church can we have communion?

When Tom asked why they weren't allowed to take communion, Angelo asked Tom to trade places with him at the table so Angelo could be facing the wall. Then he told his story. And Tom found out that this super tough guy was trying to tell Tom he was gay. Angelo ended with the question, "What does your church think of us?"

Tom pulled out his small New Testament and read the baptismal passage to Angelo. Tom told him, "It doesn't matter if you are from Juarez, a gang leader, gay or straight. The same words Jesus heard pronounced over him at his baptism, "You are my beloved.", these are the words for you. You are loved by God. The story we have at the core of our being is that we are beloved.

Angelo was now crying and said that this was the first time he had ever been told he was beloved. He got up from the table and came around to Tom. When Tom stood, Angelo wrapped his arms around Tom whispering, "That's all I needed to hear."

Tom saw Angelo the next Friday. But, then, by the following Friday Angelo was missing. Friends said he had gone out of town. Then Tom got a call from Angelo's mother, and in broken English she told Tom that Angelo had gotten out of his truck, and when crossing the street was hit by a car. She said that Angelo had told her Tom was his padre and she asked Tom to do his service.

Tom drove to Hendersonville to their double-wide mobile home. The house and yard were filled with people - family, friends, workers. Angelo's mother asked Tom if they could have the service in his church. Tom responded that since Angelo and she were Catholic, he would see if he could find a Catholic church where they could have a service. However, the local churches did not know what to do with 200 people, gang members and police included.

Angelo's mother had her Roman Catholic missal and Tom had his Book of Common Prayer. So, along with Angelo's father and a friend, they planned a service which also included some gang rituals, and decided to hold the service in the parking lot near the Denny's, where Angelo had first heard that he was beloved. The family drew a giant large chalk circle and had all the cars pulled up around that circle. It was a cathedral of headlights filled with the sounds of the sacred music that Tom had collected from them. After the service they processed in their vehicles, with headlights on, down Patton Avenue.

Later a police officer came to Tom and asked if Tom had done the service, and if he would do the same service again if called upon. He let Tom know that Angelo had recently asked the sheriff when the next officer staff meeting was, and if he could speak to them.

He was told when the next meeting was, and he showed up. He told the group that Tom had said he was beloved; and if he was beloved, they were, too. He confessed to them that he had beaten officers and trashed their cars. He apologized to them and asked their forgiveness. Several of them were at his funeral.

Tom's story is of how a man's awakening to his belovedness in God spread through gang members and police, because a priest was open to going into unknown territory in search of green corn tortillas, and to follow God's lead wherever it took him.

# SO MUCH...SO LITTLE

*Ham Fuller*

The Rev. Ham Fuller and the Rev. Bill Whisenhunt, Rector of Trinity had a long friendship which began when they were classmates at seminary. When Ham retired from full-time ministry in 2007, Bill called him to a part-time position at Trinity. After a time at Trinity, Ham was asked by Bill to serve instead as vicar of Church of the Advocate. In December of 2008 Ham was appointed to serve as vicar by Bishop Porter Taylor.

With Ham came change. Because of his years of experience as the rector of well-established parishes, the way that Church of the Advocate was organized and the scope of ministry began to evolve. He was a charismatic leader and had a long history of successfully enlisting people to engage in ministry. He was also known to be a skillful fundraiser. He very much wanted good things to happen for people who had so little, and gave himself fully to caring for the people who came through the Red Door.

Because of Ham's expansive personality and extensive experience in running large parishes, it came naturally for him to envision new initiatives for the Advocate. He was described as being "the ringmaster of the ongoings at the Advocate" and "chief cook and bottle washer of all that happened at Church of the Advocate." From all accounts, it appears that he enthusiastically initiated new projects, some of which simply could not be sustained.

The Rev. Deacon Peggy Buchanan was serving at Trinity and her diaconal ministry extended to Church of the Advocate. Since Peggy's career had been as a registered nurse, she set up a nursing cabinet and was available to guests each week for first aid and nursing advice. Peggy became less involved at the Advocate during the interim time after Ham left. However, she continued through 2022 to serve both in worship and in nursing care after her retirement from active ministry as a deacon.

Congregations in the Diocese continued with their generous donations of food. They were further engaged by Ham to donate clothing, and a clothing closet was begun. As activities increased, parish groups stepped up to the plate with financial support and volunteers.

Ham got busy applying for grants and organizing fundraisers. Church of the Advocate was in the diocesan budget, which provided for the part-time vicar's salary. All ministries and activities were dependent upon grants and fundraisers. Most of what was received by the Advocate in terms of food, clothing, personal and medical supplies, was donated.

Ham saw the need for individuals who were typically unemployable to have a way to enter into meaningful work. He did a study with the folks who attended the Advocate to learn about their educational levels, background, and what they needed. He sought out service projects, provided volunteers from the Church of the Advocate, and then paid them cash under the table.

A new, but short-lived, venture was the creation of StreetWafels. Ham procured a machine to make traditional Stroopwafels in order to provide employment. A website was developed and orders were placed mainly by supportive congregations.

Thanksgiving meals and Christmas parties were a big deal. In a newspaper article Ham likened himself and his truck filled with donations to Santa Claus and his sleigh, as he collected large amounts of clothing and supplies and found joy in giving them to those in need. There was an annual Christmas party, that included a traditional meal, gifts and shoes – all covered by donations.

While the meals provided by parishes continued, Ham signed the Advocate up with Manna FoodBank so that the kitchen could be stocked with staples and qualify for kitchen equipment. Ham got local restaurants engaged in donating food. However, the demand upon volunteers to pick up these donations on a weekly basis proved to be unsustainable.

Joining with members at St. Luke's Episcopal Church in Boone, North Carolina, Ham made it possible for a group of unhoused people from the Advocate to travel to the gulf coast to volunteer after Hurricane Katrina.

The Sunday worship style was to gather in a very casual, loosely formed circle. The intentional circle of trust with carefully crafted liturgical worship had fallen by the wayside. Some individuals, who considered themselves street preachers, assumed the role of preacher. With people trickling in and out, some participating, some not engaged at all, the setting was very chaotic. There were drug deals, outbursts and police being called. The Red Door had become the location of a lot of dangerous activity.

From people's reports, it seems that it all became too much for Ham to handle. Perhaps he was trying to overlay the robustness of his former ministry settings onto the Advocate. But, in aspiring to swell the Advocate into a larger operation, to make more of a difference for more people, he had overextended himself and others.

Included in Ham's obituary, after his death on April 10, 2017, are these words:

> Ham lived out his love of God and of people wherever he went, sharing encouragement and celebrating the possibilities and blessings of life in God... One of the great joys of his life was the ministry to the homeless of the Church of the Advocate.... In lieu of flowers contributions to Ham's memory may be made to the Church of the Advocate.

*Ham Fuller*

*Ham and men from Advocate laying hands on the van they used*

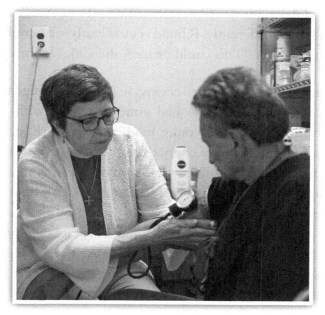

*Peggy Buchanan providing nursing care*

# THIS COULD BE ME

*Rhonda Candler Kilby*

Rhonda and Eugene Kilby came to be involved with Church of the Advocate through their parish church, which was on the Sunday meal schedule to prepare and deliver meals about four times a year.

Rhonda immediately felt a connection at the Advocate. She and Eugene found their eyes and hearts opened to the people they encountered there. "It was like scales falling off our eyes," she said, as they began to see differently. Rhonda could easily see herself in some of the people's faces. "This could be me," she said, "or my children."

One Sunday when they were serving at Advocate, Eugene had an epiphany. A young man who had gone to school with their son came in for a meal. As the young man came up to Eugene to say hello, Eugene immediately recognized him. Any perception Eugene may have had about the homeless and hungry existing in a different reality from his own, dissolved before his eyes. When Rhonda, who had worked locally as registered nurse, would be downtown, she would see people she recognized from the Advocate that she had also seen previously in a clinical setting. They were not a category unto themselves, but had come from all walks of life, and were members of the same community as Rhonda and Eugene.

Rhonda was deeply devoted to the ministry. In 2016, with Ham's departure, Rhonda, stepped into the void. As needs arose, she responded. Since she was a registered nurse, she provided nursing care when Peggy Buchanan couldn't be there. When the treasurer moved on, she handled the financial tasks. She gave direction and support to the office manager. She made order out of the chaos. She simplified things that had become unmanageable. The clothes closet had grown into big containers of clothes that were impossible to sort and clean. She got rid of the clothes and kept the shoe closet, Sole Mates, and the daily personal supplies which became known as The Basics.

Rhonda was asked to step into formal leadership at Advocate and remained involved until 2022. During Rhonda's first year, an art center was added. The Red Door was unlocked at noon on Sundays. As people came in through the Red Door, they were welcomed in and invited to rest and get a cup of coffee and a snack, and enjoy what the art center had to offer. On the art table were large pre-printed murals that people could color and decorate. Greeting cards and stamps were available so people could connect with their families. The art center also served as a quiet place to write. For a time, the table was hosted by a man who, through his own talents, guided people in creating art that was expressive of their lives, their stories. Most of those who came to the art table would stay for the worship service, which began at 1:30, followed by lunch.

Rhonda says that involvement at Advocate continued to be an abiding source of energy for her and was central to her own spiritual life. As she got more and more involved, she found that being in this context helped her to discern her personal motives and theology.

During Rhonda's time, the idea of providing work experience continued to present itself as a goal. A few regular members were hired to work on Sundays to set up chairs for worship and work in the kitchen. A concept began to take shape in Rhonda's mind and she developed the Good Works! Program. This program was created for individuals who are not ready to seek paying jobs in the community. They may be facing obstacles such as homelessness, living with addiction, trying to manage mental health issues, dealing with unhealthy relationships, and more.

Rhonda would arrange for crew members to work as volunteers for area agencies such as Habitat for Humanity and local conference centers; for churches that have building and grounds projects; and for individuals who have house or yard work. Crew members learned skills such as good communication and dependability. They were paid a fair hourly wage, the funds coming from grants and donations. As they developed a good work ethic and a belief in themselves, the hope was that their stability and quality of life would increase.

Rhonda set up the program in this way:

After meeting with a licensed counselor and the program coordinator, each person must establish a checking account, have a cell phone, and if not housed, be in the application process for housing. A local bank supports the program by allowing the crew members to open checking accounts with no service fees. If the person doesn't have a cell phone, one is provided until the first paycheck is deposited.

To be on the Good Works! Crew each person must meet weekly with a professional counselor provided by the Advocate, also paid through grants. The counselor and program coordinator work with each person to develop a plan to improve life skills, self-care, and employment goals. Housing is an important goal because survival becomes a full-time job for someone sleeping outside and seeking out the basic necessities each day. It is hard to be unhoused and have the stability to be committed to regular work.

Through this program individuals have the opportunity to begin to integrate into a supportive work environment and to experience hope for real and positive change. Those who welcome the crew members into the workplace or work project are given the opportunity to know the crew members as individuals and see their contributions, which lowers the stereotype often placed upon people who are unhoused and unemployed. A dependable van is needed to transport the crew members to the work sites.

Rhonda mentioned that they used to limit how long people could work on Crew. Crew membership was originally limited to two 12-week cycles; then to a year. As the program progressed, Rhonda realized that, while some crew members were able to graduate into regular employment, there are those individuals who need to remain in the program long-term. They many not be employable, but they have found meaningful work and belonging in a supportive community to be life-changing. And, they have become an integral part of the community that is formed through the Advocate and the Good Works! Program.

When asked about street ministry, Rhonda said that the Red Door no longer had a regular presence out on the streets like it did in the early days, but it continues to reach out at some level. Communion continues to be offered on Sundays to the people outside the Red Door. On Ash Wednesday, prayers and ashes are offered to people on the streets of downtown Asheville. One recent priest has reached out to the local jail and another has visited the homeless camps. When youth were there in summer, they would be taken on a walking tour through downtown. As the youths handed out water bottles to those in the park and on the sidewalks, they were exposed to the complexities of homelessness and the diversity among the unhoused.

Rhonda said that the landscape of being homeless in downtown Asheville has changed drastically over the past twenty years. For a long time, Church of the Advocate was noted as the most established ministry to the homeless. Now there are several well-established agencies. Homeward Bound is working to prevent and end homelessness through permanent housing and support. AHOPE, with whom the early vicars kept a relationship, continues to provide daily support and services to the unhoused. ABCCM

(Asheville Buncombe County Christian Ministry), with its Veterans Restoration Quarters and Transformation Village, is successfully providing transitional housing.

BeLoved Asheville's website offers this succinct description of their abiding ministry in Asheville: "BeLoved constantly is in the "eye of the storm" providing for those in need and helping us to remember the humanity in all." (belovedasheville.com) They go out into the community to meet the needs they find there. Their current work includes building microhomes, providing medics on the streets, food sharing, racial justice, and more.

The Haywood Street Congregation was founded in 2009 as a mission of the United Methodist Church. Like Church of the Advocate, it began with the vision of the institutional Church serving Jesus by reinventing itself to seek out the most excluded in society and develop programming to serve their needs and build relationships with them so they can discover their belonging and worth in the family of God. It has continued through the years to grow into its mission. (haywoodstreet.org)

Rhonda named an area of need that might be well-fitted to Church of the Advocate - a relational ministry with people who are newly housed. Finally having a place to call home can be a true miracle after the long wait and all the paper work involved. But, having a roof overhead and being enclosed in four walls after living on the streets can be disorienting and lonely. A stigma forms as the newly housed begin to live separate lives from those who are unhoused. Since forming beloved community is at the heart of being Church, connecting with neighbors who are living alone is a natural.

In closing, Rhonda talked about the presence of Church of the Advocate in the Diocese and the local community. "We are a bridge, a thin place, holy ground. We can serve to connect people who give money and drop off things at the door to the gospel imperative of self-giving love. We are a place where Jesus's teachings can be incarnated. How can we create a way for Church of the Advocate to engage people to come in further to the fertile ground of experiencing and participating in the Realm of God?"

*Rhonda in the kitchen with Chris Kamm*

*Crew members working at Lake Logan*

# JESUS WELCOMES YOU!

*Brother John Huebner*

Brother John Huebner, a Franciscan Missioner, moved to Asheville in 2012. The Order of St. Francis is a brotherhood of like-minded men who follow St. Francis' example as a discipline in service to God. They are an order that exists apostolically: the brothers are embedded in the world with normal lives, rather than enclosed in a monastery. They live in different parts of the world, each with their own individual ministry, based upon the needs of their respective local communities and parishes. (orderofsaintfrancis.org)

As a Franciscan Missioner, Brother John immediately reached out into the local community to find a ministry context. He met with Vicar Ham Fuller to learn about the Red Door. Ham invited John to their Tuesday bible study and asked him to gradually take it over. At that point Ham was struggling to fulfill the demands of the ministry. Soon afterward John received a phone call from Rhonda, that Ham was going on an extended leave of absence. She asked John if he would take over on Tuesdays and participate in Sunday worship. And with that, John became more fully engaged in ministry at the Advocate.

Just as Rhonda stepped into leadership in administration and program, John naturally put his energy into worship and formation. John changed the Tuesday Bible Study to a Lectio Divina format in which a portion of scripture is read three times, with silence between each reading. After each reading the participants in the circle are invited to share 1) a word of phrase that speaks to them; 2) why they think God is nudging them to pay attention to this word or phrase; 3) how they hope their lives will be informed and changed. Taize chants and healing prayer with anointing were gradually incorporated. The Prayer Circle, as it is called, became a sacred place in which wisdom and belonging once again were the hallmarks of gathering at the Advocate.

Rhonda and John were talking on a Tuesday about the large cross that hung behind the altar. It was made of sharp jagged wood with a barbed wire crown of thorns. It had been made by a veteran in the early days to represent the hard lives of many who came to the Red Door. While it remains in the room, John and Rhonda remarked that the people who come to the Red Door have lives that are jagged enough and decided to smooth the edges and have the altar space speak more of safety and beauty and peace.

The altar was moved to a side wall, further away from the entrance. Rhonda had a card of an icon named *The Resurrected Christ* which portrays a risen Jesus with arms extended in a gesture of welcome. A perfect icon for the Advocate altar! John found out who had rights to it, Conception Abbey in Conception, Missouri. John wrote a letter to the nun who had created the icon, Sister Marie-Paul Farran. He explained the ministry, and got her permission to have the icon photographed and enlarged. John also arranged to have his brother make wooden altar candlesticks to match the altar, an aumbry with a Jerusalem cross etched on the glass door to remember the sister who wrote the altar icon, and a sanctuary lamp.

After Ham left, supply clergy came in on Sundays. Vic Mansfield, who had just retired as rector of a local parish, became the regular supply priest. The worship service on Sunday had lost its structure and the peace and belonging of the circle was missing. It was no easy task, but Vic brought order back into worship. As John said, "Vic cleaned it up. He knew how to handle outbursts and bad behavior. He was excellent in relating to the people who came to the Red Door. The whole structure on Sunday mornings changed. It was wonderful to see. Worship that was relevant and liturgical returned."

Brother John and Rhonda met with the new Bishop of the Diocese of Western North Carolina, José McLaughlin, as soon as he arrived. John, Rhonda and José were in agreement that Church of the Advocate was first and foremost to be a place of spiritual feeding. Because of this John continued his intentionality in shaping the worship service and the worship space. John began offering anointing on Sundays. Altar linens and candles were added to the altar. The deacon at the time, Clare Barry, was given a more active role in liturgy. A processional cross was added. Each Sunday, Vic Mansfield would start with a kind of instructional eucharist by explaining the procession – Jesus was always on the move and we are always following Jesus. He would draw attention to the Gospel reading by explaining that the stories of Jesus are so important that we put them in a special book. The first gospel book was donated by Clare Barry. John arranged for a set of altar frontals to be made in honor of women who had contributed to the ministry of the Red Door. They are Clare Barry, Rhonda Candler Kilby, Liz Minor, Nicki Peresich, and Dena Whalen.

Rhonda and the Board worked with Bishop José to bring stability into the interim situation. Vic's status as supply priest eventually changed to that of interim vicar. Meanwhile the Board worked on the discernment of God's will for Church of the Advocate, what the scope of its ministry should include, and what kind of leadership was needed. Scott White, the rector of Trinity, became more involved, offering guidance to the Board and encouraging Trinity's support of Advocate.

Sarah Woods was called in March 2019 to serve as vicar. At that time the worship at Church of the Advocate and the Good Works!

Crew were running well. Church of the Advocate now had two clear and evident purposes – a safe place for spiritual growth, including worship in the Episcopal tradition, and the Good Works! Program. While Sarah was at the Advocate for a very short time, she had a pastoral and motherly touch which brought about the quality of belovedness for everyone involved. She and Brother John raised the money needed to take the kids at the Advocate on youth trips in a new van, obtained through generous grants. They engaged the kids in worship as acolytes and lectors and offered them the opportunity to go to Camp Henry, the summer camp in the Diocese of Western North Carolina.

When Sarah left, supply priests were once again scheduled. Deacon Tim Ervolina was assigned by Bishop José to the Advocate during yet another interim time. Tim brought administrative and fundraising skills as well as a genuine concern for the people who came through the Red Door. He was passionate about the gospel, preaching a stirring sermon and then practicing what he preached. He could present himself as a well-healed cleric at a meeting and then don his T-shirt and his bandana and head out to the streets to meet with people there.

John tells a story about a woman named Nicky Peresich, with whom he developed a pastoral friendship. She had volunteered for years at the Advocate. There was a middle-eastern man who attended the Advocate seasonally. Whenever this man came into the Red Door he would be drawn to the icon behind the altar. One day, after being away for some time, he entered the Red Door and asked where Nicky was. He told John, "Nicky is like my relative, the one here that really cares for me." He and Nicky were both Eastern Orthodox, which helps explain why he was drawn to Nicky and to the icon. The man opened his wallet and pulled out a worn photo of Nicky and showed it to John. He said he carried it wherever he went. John, in turn, got a photo made of this young man standing with Nicky and waited for the day he could give it to him. After a time, John ran into the young man. Tears of gratitude filled his eyes when John handed him the photo.

Nicky's healing presence was missed at the Advocate as she suffered serious health issues. John began regular visits to her home, taking communion and treats she could enjoy.

During the COVID shut-down, John knew Nicky and her son would need food. He began, and continues, to take groceries and communion. Nicky has also become very close to John's son and her face lights up when John's son joins him for the visits.

For ten years Brother John faithfully continued to lead the Tuesday Prayer Circle and to minister to various individuals who were part of the Red Door community. He joyfully called everyone to witness God's love in action. In everything he did at the Advocate, he sought to enhance the healing, wholeness, peace, and serenity that he believed it was meant to house.

He hopes that the future for Church of the Advocate will include building more connections for the Holy Spirit to work through the collective ministries for the unhoused, marginalized, and working poor in Asheville.

He believes that the symbols and sacred stories present in Episcopal worship can serve to feed the souls that hunger and thirst for places of order and beauty, that hold the presence of Jesus, the presence of the Holy. For anyone who comes through the Red Door, he believes that the chaos of the streets can give way to a setting that feeds the soul as well as the body. Says John, "Taste, touch, smell, sight, texture, candles, incense, oil, human connectedness. These hold the Presence in the space."

As a Franciscan Missioner John knows he must discern when the wind of the Holy Spirit has shifted and it is time to follow Jesus into a new ministry. He now serves as a pastoral visitor to the sick and recovering.

# THE ICON

*The Resurrected Christ* icon has become a well-known symbol for Church of the Advocate. This description of the icon is summarized from the website of The Printery House. (www.printeryhouse.org)

Christ appears in a robe of brilliant white, recalling his radiant garments at the Transfiguration. "And he was transfigured before them, and his face shown like the sun, and his clothes became dazzling white (Matthew 17:2)." White was also the color of the robes of the righteous in John's Revelation and, through the ages, white robes have symbolized membership in the Church, gained through baptism.

Jesus' arms are opened wide in a gesture of welcome but also displaying the wounds of his crucifixion. Surrounding his head is a halo, signifying sanctity. His halo includes a cross and the Greek letters omicron, omega and nu, meaning "Who Am" or roughly translated "the one who is", the name used for God in Exodus 3:14. Sister Marie-Paul Farran, the writer of the icon purposely darkened the skin and narrowed the facial features of Jesus to reflect an Aramaic speaking Jew. Jesus' gaze is serious and focused, as in most icons, but full of warmth and compassion.

The background of the icon is gold leaf. Gold has traditionally been used to symbolize divine light because the metallic surface reflects and enriches light that strikes it in a manner so different from paint. The letters on the background, IC XC, are the Greek monogram for Christ, the first and last letters in the Greek words for Jesus and Christ, Iesous Khristos. The oval shape surrounding Christ is called a mandorla which represents an opening ripped asunder in the fabric of the world to expose the glory of heaven beyond, symbolic of divine revelation.

Each Sunday and Tuesday that John would welcome people, he would stand in front of the altar with the icon behind him when he called those gathered to prepare for worship. In imitation of Jesus' wide open and inviting arms, Br. John would open his arms wide and with his bright smile would say, "Welcome! Jesus has been waiting for you!"

*Icon of The Resurrected Christ*

*John with Nicky*

*John leading Tuesday Prayer & Healing Circle*

*John explaining Lectio Divina*

*Bishop Jose helping prep a meal*

*Vic Mansfield imposing Ash Wednesday ashes on the streets of Asheville*

*Vic leading worship in courtyard of Trinity*

*Sarah Woods with youth group on summer trip*

*Deacon Tim Ervolina*

*Tim's tireless oversight of food ministry*

# A SAFETY NET

*Crewmembers*

Over the span of a few years a man we'll call Dan would occasionally drop in at the Red Door. Eventually, he began to make a concentrated effort to be there every Sunday. What caused him to return to the Red Door and then stay and join the GoodWorks! Crew? He says it was a progressive combination of things. When he was on the street, the attraction was being able to get in somewhere, get his backpack off his back, get off his feet and relax for three or four hours. He came in to get out of the weather, to get a good meal, to be around people. He began to stay because he found a sense of safety, peace, and compassion. For him, this was what set the Church of the Advocate apart from other service providers. This has been the pattern for many who have become members of GoodWorks!.

When asked what was the glue that began to hold things together for them, one person replied, "Because I kept coming here, some bonds were beginning to be formed. Time spent here every week made it safe to share about my life and my feelings about family issues. Relationships were building as I kept coming back. People here were looking past my faults. We believe in you. We want to be there for you. People at the Red Door remember what's going on in people's lives, like asking 'How did your doctor visit go?'. It meant something to know that they knew about the little things going on in my life."

Another crew member remarked, "Because of the nurturing, I felt comfortable being honest about what was going on, like needing money to wash clothes. I didn't think of it as them enabling me, but that they gave respect to my needs."

Worship at the Advocate, for some, took some getting used to. One person said she was born Catholic, which she remembered as too structured and dogmatic. Another grew up in a charismatic Pentecostal church which he found very emotionally driven and unsettling. As they got accustomed to the Episcopal liturgy at the Advocate, they both agreed that they were attracted to how involved they felt during worship. Everyone had the choice to participate or stay on the outer edge and observe. The word of God was preached in practical ways; how to use God's word in an everyday sense; not high unreachable ideals they couldn't reach.

During the Covid shut-down, even though work projects were not possible, the crew members stayed faithful to serving on Sundays. The meals now had to be plated in to-go containers, bagged up and rolled on carts out into Trinity's Aston Street courtyard. Serving tables, a disinfectant/hand washing station, and a large cart that held daily supplies provided to people were hauled outside. Later, when outdoor worship was allowed, they took the altar and chairs into the courtyard each Sunday. Then, everything would be brought back in, and they helped clean and disinfect the kitchen and mop the floors.

Some individuals worked on crew for awhile and then would move on. One happy success story involved a man who worked on crew during Covid. As the restrictions lifted and Rhonda returned as director of Good Works!, the community work opportunities opened back up. This man was given leadership responsibilities when the crew worked at various local non-profits. He was then chosen by the Kitchen Manager to assist in the kitchen on Sundays. When the Kitchen Manager resigned, he recommended that this man be considered for the position. He earned his SafeServ certificate and as the new Kitchen Manager he took on new responsibilities. He coordinated with Food Connections to receive donated food. He purchased food and kitchen supplies, kept the pantry stocked, rotated frozen and shelved foods, and prepared the weekly meals. He also oversaw the maintenance of the Red Door van.

Being on the Good Works! Crew can challenge individuals who have worked sporadically or at day labor jobs. Those who are caught in addiction look for jobs that fit around their usage and they learn strategies for avoiding drug testing. Although work crew members are never required to attend worship services, they must be accountable for weekly counselor appointments, crew meetings and work crew assignments. Those who stick with the requirements to be in the Good Works! Program say they find community and self-respect within the supportive structure.

One woman said, "Rhonda became a big mentor to me in regard to remembering how to behave on job sites, how to treat people, how to act in social settings, how to be trustworthy, how to do things in a proper procedure; soft skills – being on time, working hard while you're there. She helped me to realize what it takes to be on a job site; the moral aspects of working with other people. She set that standard for all the crew members. She walked a pretty tight rope with all that. She was strict!"

It wasn't unusual for men and women who were in the Good Works! Program to stay clean from addiction, work the program, see the counselor each week, and then fall back into using. While some left the program permanently, unable to kick tenacious addictions, others would return to try again.

When one man was aware of the absence and relapse of a crewmember, he said, "It broke my heart. A person can have so many positive things going on. The guilt associated with the relapse will keep them from coming back to the Red Door at first. But when they step back through the Red Door, there is the safety net waiting for them, holding them up while they continue to try to find their whole and true self."

One person opened up about his return to the Red Door. We asked him why he had stayed away from us for so long. He talked about all his losses in life. Because of his addiction to drugs, he had done some bad things and gone to jail. He lost his wife and became estranged from his son. His behavior caused his father and his brother and sister to distance themselves from him.

He said how *hard it was* to come back to church because he felt like we would see him for who he was. And, that we wouldn't want anything to do with him. He expected to be unwelcome, marginalized, and not trusted. He had let everyone down and that's what he deserved.

But, when he did return and everyone rejoiced and embraced him, kind of like the story of the prodigal son, he said he felt like he must be worth something to be treated like that. He said that was what Church was supposed to be all about - people deciding to love – and to love those who don't deserve love – because that is how God loves. He said, "I'm here for keeps because every time I come through that red door, I am reminded without a doubt that I'm loveable - loved by God. You all remind me that I'm wanted here and welcomed."

He said it was because he had been welcomed back and his needs for help were met with respect and concern, and because the counselor helped him process his family dynamics, that he got up the courage to contact his dad. And before too long, he and his dad were meeting for dinner and even playing golf together. When Christmas came around, he and his brother and sister reunited.

When Easter came around, he wanted to publicly reaffirm his baptismal vows because, he said, he had been on the receiving end of God's love and now he wanted to be on the giving end of God's love.

Someone said that the biggest thing that helps them stay committed to being on Crew, even when they make mistakes, was to know they could be honest with people at the Red Door. Another person commented, "When people see you go through the same things with no change, they tend to turn their backs on you. I didn't get that here. People cared more about me than the mistakes I was making. Because of this I could still have hope. This place was a catalyst, a steady encourager."

Several of the crewmembers agreed that being in a community of faith helped them begin to see beyond their own problems to the larger context of efforts going on to make a difference in people's lives. One said, "This ministry is more important than what I'm going through. Advocate wasn't just saying they were making a difference – they really were."

A crewmember gave an example as he described a man who was also on the work crew, and was a regular member of the Advocate on Sundays and Tuesdays. "He recently almost died in the woods. People from here stepped outside of themselves. We've got to stay connected to him. They went to see him at the hospital, helped him take care of details. Br. John went every Tuesday to pick him up at Haywood Congregation's Respite Care to bring him to the Prayer Circle."

When asked about the hallmark, the charism, of the Church of the Advocate, one person readily answered, "It's this simple: What goes on at the Advocate is what the love of Christ actually looks like. The only other times I had encountered this acceptance was when I received it from God himself. The value I've been given at the Red Door is the value we all have in Christ. There were times in my life when I had plenty of money and success, yet I always wanted more – cars, nice places, spending lots of money. And my wants always left me wanting more. I know God wants us to be free of this wanting. In this community I experienced a freedom to be fully alive physically and spiritually that reminded me that I could seek that freedom for myself. I like the word liberty – it is something that I have to struggle to achieve. Drawing closer to God is about becoming liberated from this carnal superficiality."

When asked about positive changes in their lives since joining GoodWorks!, various crewmembers responded: I have gone through a gamut of transitions. My health is much improved. I have a roof over my head. I've gone back to college. I've advanced in my job. My family connections are stronger. I'm taking better care of myself. I'm discovering what my interests are in life, what I want out of a relationship. I've paid off my debts.

As to the future of the Advocate, here is one response: "I have high hopes for GoodWorks!. Weekly group meetings are required. They are an anchor in our week and keep communication going. As for the next step, I hope there will be more involvement in terms of helping the crew members transition from old ways into a better life. I would like to see us more involved in their daily lives; to help them successfully deal with personal issues and to build more community among the team."

Another response: "The Good Works! program is something that makes sense. This program/ministry is a very established and rooted part of the local community. It means something. It is helping to change lives. That makes a difference to people. It meant something to me. I've been in programs that didn't last and the bottom fell out. If this program has abided up to now, something is working; something is right about this. This isn't just an experiment that is trying to fix something. It is an established part of the community. The entire enterprise of the Church of the Advocate is not just about what we're doing. It is our *being* in the community – a presence that is the hands and heart of Christ, in the love of God."

Another person hopes there will be better use of the van. "Church of the Advocate is both inside the Red Door and beyond it. The van as a symbol and a means of *going with* people. An increase in transportation services is "not just as transportation but as the relationship that goes with people in improving their options."

*GoodWorks! Crew at work on the steep slopes at St. Matthias*

# GOD GOT MY ARMOR OFF

*Dereck Moody*

Dereck is the first one to tell you that he was a person who was filled with anger, was empty of trust, and not easily approached. As Dereck began to come to the Advocate regularly on Sundays and Tuesdays, he joined the work crew, and met weekly with the counselor. He admits that, at first, he signed on to earn some cash. Then, he began to believe he could trust the place.

He has shared some of his past, revealing that his mother abandoned him and his grandfather took him in and raised him. His uncles have been a constant, long-distance supportive presence in his life. He has sometimes lived with people who took him in, and other times he has been unhoused. He has been able to work in landscaping until recently. His ability to work has been hindered by emphysema and C.O.P.D.

Dereck says that because of his counselor, and Tim and Dena as his pastors, he slowly began to let his armor come off. As he became more involved, he became protective of the Red Door, acting as an usher, or sometimes you might say, a bouncer. He welcomed people and sometimes warned the staff about potential dangers. He continues to watch out after people on the street whom he met at the Advocate and enthusiastically tries keeps them connected.

Dereck had a bad infection in his teeth and gums. When asked if he wanted help, he said yes and got the dental care he needed and new dentures. When it was noticed that he couldn't read the shoe sizes in the Sole Mates closet, he was asked if he wanted to have his eyes checked. He said yes and glasses were provided. When asked if he wanted to be baptized and take his place in the church, he said yes and was baptized. When asked if he wanted a home of his own, he said yes and was guided through the initial paperwork by a social worker who was working at the Advocate on Sundays. He is now living independently in his own apartment and is enrolled in Medicaid.

If you ask him how he is, most of the time he will say without hesitation, "God is good and I am blessed. Because of the Red Door, God got my armor off, softened me up, gave me new teeth, got me baptized, and set me up in my own place. I try to bless somebody every day. I'm good at getting people to laugh."

*Dereck with Tim enjoying pancakes*

# TURNED UPSIDE DOWN
# AND LEVELED

*A Volunteer*

This woman wishes to remain anonymous and we will know her as Ann. At first, Ann came as a volunteer to the bible studies on Tuesdays and continued to attend her own church on Sundays. In time, she led some small prayer groups and then got involved with the annual fundraisers.

What kept bringing her back? She heard in the voice of people, who shared about their lives and their spiritual journeys, an authenticity and openness which deeply touched her. As she became more aware of what a hard life they had growing up – a lack of role models, support, and stability – she was newly awakened to the blessings in her life. Without the foundation of love and self-worth she had received all her life, she wondered what her life would have been like.

She became close to one woman whose young son died while he was in foster care. People from Trinity came forward spontaneously when the Advocate announced that there would be a memorial service. They provided flowers and a reception and their own presence at the service. The young mother told Ann she had never felt so loved by people who didn't know her.

She also remarked how meaningful it was for her son to have been given a memorial service. In the unstable world of homelessness and poverty so many people die with no funeral, no remembrance. Ann mentioned that she keeps the boy's photo on her shelf – for all the children whose photos have never graced a home.

Ann's involvement at the Advocate turned her stereotypes upside down. A man who regularly suffered from psychiatric problems would at times be brilliant in his insights during bible study. When she received the communion cup from a homeless man, the vast differences in their two lives were leveled. One day when she was preoccupied about something, a homeless man, without knowing what troubled her, came up behind her and kissed her on the top of her head and said, "You're gonna be alright."

Ann found it very comforting to be with people who "lived at the bottom of the world." They were so real as they dealt with their heavy problems. During this time at the Advocate, she also felt like she was at the bottom of the world because a beloved family member was sinking in addiction. Because she felt safe sharing during the Tuesday Prayer Circle, Ann allowed herself to be vulnerable and speak her truth.

As she spilled her heart out, a man in the group leaned forward and said, "Girl, you gotta let go! You've only given God one hand and you're holding on to the other one. Let go of her so God can have both of her hands!" Ann knew that God had spoken to her through this man. Even though this man probably didn't know where he would sleep that night or get his next meal, he was completely attentive and freely gave her his all in that moment.

As Ann got to know other volunteers, she recognized that some of them, too, were drawn to the holy ground of the Advocate because of the same authenticity and non-judgment she had experienced. She said, "Together, we supported each other and felt grounded. We learned that we could be compassionate with those we love and keep boundaries at the same time."

Toward the end of the interview, Ann offered this insight.

"When I was focused in on my pain, I was looking through a little microscope and all I could see were my troubles and my pain. Getting to know the people at the Advocate opened up my pain to embrace the pain in the world, so evident in their lives, and to realize how small my pain is in the larger view. The pain shrinks when you open up to the wider scope of the pain in the world. If I make myself vulnerable to the pain around me, I learn to open up to my own pain. That's when the healing begins."

*Crew members leading prayer during the memorial service for a crew member's child.*

# MAY I HELP YOU?

*Bill Dockendorf*

Bill and his wife Jan moved to Asheville in 2012. They became members of Trinity in 2013 and he got involved with the Advocate in 2013. Ham Fuller was the vicar at the time. He asked Bill to go to lunch and explained the ministry of the Advocate. At that time, Ham was trying to structure an advisory board and asked Bill if he would serve on it. With a background as a business owner, Bill naturally honed in on the organizational and financial aspects of the ministry.

Bill and Rhonda became board members at the same time. Soon after Bill and Rhonda became board members, Ham exited. The Advisory Board knew they needed to raise money. They organized their first annual fundraiser, with several more to follow.

Bill worked with Rhonda to start the first work crew. To get the program off the ground they needed a means of transportation for the crew. Bill went to his neighborhood's members association, which awarded grants each year, and appealed for a van. Rhonda set up the crew program. Their goal from the beginning was to "give people a sense of achievement, a stake in their own life, a sense of self-dignity."

When Rhonda had to take leave for medical reasons, Bill carried on raising funds, took the task of treasurer, and called the board meetings.

Bill remembers that the board's understanding of the Advocate's main purpose was to have worship at its center and to provide a place two days a week where people on the street could come, be welcomed and get a meal. Bill, as a board member, always sought to engage with the guests as much as possible.

One Sunday Bill took notice of a teenage boy, about fourteen years old, sitting quietly by himself. He wore a work crew T-shirt and, not knowing how easy or difficult it would be, Bill thought he would try to engage him. Jaden was his name. He, his sister, Evony, and their grandmother, Natalie attended on Sundays. During this time, Natalie was awarded guardianship of Jaden and Evony. The Red Door had been suggested to Natalie and she began attending the Sunday worship and meal when Jaden was 11 and Evony was 8. All three were part of the work crew for a time.

The Red Door had been suggested to Natalie and she began attending the Sunday worship and meal when Jaden was 11 and Evony was 8.

Natalie reflected on what it was like to go to Advocate. "It felt like you were somebody, not looked down on. It was the first and only church I've gone to in Asheville. At first Ham was the pastor. I was very taken with him. And Sarah Woods was so good with Evony. Brother John took the kids on fun trips, and his son, Josh, and Jaden became good friends. Chris Kamm spent time each week with Jaden, taking him on long bicycle rides and getting him strong. He gave Jaden a good outlook on life.

"As the kids and I continued to go there, we grew stronger in the community and it was something the three of us did together every week. Being a member of the crew was wonderful. Rhonda had it all organized and paid attention to each one of us. It was good being able to be with people and accomplish something with them. The counselor could brighten my outlook on life. I would show up feeling low and come out with a smile on my face. When the kids and I were finally able to move from my studio apartment into a townhouse with three bedrooms, everybody from the Red Door, Br. John, Dena, the work crew, helped us move and got us the furniture we needed."

Now fourteen years old and in high school, Evony easily listed favorite memories during her six previous years at Advocate. She liked being asked to light the altar candles or carry the cross. She enjoyed being on the work crew, working alongside the adults and earning some spending money. She also attended Camp Henry two summers. She remembers lunch and shopping with Beth Chestnut, the Director of Children's Ministry at Trinity. And, while the schools were closed during Covid, she and Jaden went to Trinity each school day to attend their online classes. A team of people provided transportation every morning and every afternoon. A member of Trinity and retired math professor, Sarah Butrum, worked each week with Evony.

Jaden didn't resist Bill's initial approach, even though Bill had to pull every response out of him. It surprised Jaden the next Sunday that Bill remembered his name. They slowly built a relationship of trust. Bill tried to learn about Jaden's life. His father was in prison. His mother was not able to take care of him and his sister. His grandmother was his caregiver. Bill tried to understand what their life was like in terms of a daily reality. Through time, Bill "peeled back the onion one layer at a time." Jaden gradually opened up and Bill felt more and more compelled to help him.

Jaden was a gifted student, extremely shy, and hadn't had the opportunity to develop social skills. Bill recalls how surprised he was that Jaden had never attended a sporting event. Bill approached Jaden and said, "I want to help you with some things. I'm not being critical of you as a person, but I would like to offer you some guidance, some hints, some advice." The first goal Bill set was eye contact. "You're not used to looking at people. When they talk to you they want to talk *with* you. They are interested in you." Bill constantly encouraged Jaden to practice eye-contact with Bill and others.

Bill started picking Jaden up after school. They would go get something to eat and talk about what was going on in Jaden's life, what his goals were. Bill worked with Jaden to approach his goals as "concrete rather than abstract, short-term rather than long-term; to think of achievement as a process of attainable steps."

Bill believed in Jaden. He felt it was reasonable for Jaden to strive toward going to college. It had not occurred to Jaden as a possibility and he was afraid to want it. Bill also encouraged Jaden to get his learner's permit and helped him study for it. Then, Bill taught Jaden how to drive. Jaden gradually came to know that Bill was going to stick with him until the goal was achieved.

Bill gives Jaden's grandmother a lot of credit. "This kid is such an enigma, but he has had some good upbringing along the way. He is a respectful, constrained young man. He has not ever headed toward trouble and has a reasonable amount of self-esteem."

One day when they were driving, Bill saw a house for sale. He said to Jaden, "That's a nice house for sale. Do you think that would ever be part of your future, to buy a house and live in it?" Jaden said no. Bill said, "Don't sell yourself short. You *will* buy a house. That's what success in your academics and social life will lead to."

Jaden graduated from high school and was offered a scholarship at UNCA. And Bill is still there, cheering him on.

What are Bill's hopes for Advocate? He hopes that the Bishop and the Diocese understand the importance of ministry through the Advocate for people like Jaden and his family. He hopes that the future potential will be recognized and the ministry will be re-envisioned so as to improve and transform it. He hopes the right vicar will be called, someone who can maintain it as a priority in the community. He is grateful for Trinity's uninterrupted involvement and support of the Advocate, while the Advocate serves in a major way to enable Trinity and other parishes in the Diocese to minister to the people the Church is called to serve.

*Bill Dockendorf*

*Jaden's graduation, May 2023*

# FOR SUCH A TIME AS THIS

*Gerald Ashby*

Like Bill and Jan Dockendorf, it was retirement that brought Gerald and his wife Margaret, a Lutheran pastor, to Asheville in 2011. Gerald remembers that he had clothing to give away. When he arrived at Trinity to deliver the clothing, he asked the person who met him what else they needed and was told they needed sleeping bags and blankets. Gerald probed further. "No, what do you *really* need?" Well, we don't have any music for our Sunday service. Gerald heard this as a call from God and was told to contact Rhonda.

Gerald started showing up every Sunday with his guitar to lead music. He met Gray Pearson, a teenager at Trinity who was a gifted musician. Rhonda asked Gerald if he would coordinate the music for the Advocate, involving Gray and other potential musicians. The next Sunday, when Gerald arrived, Rhonda presented him with his new business cards – Music Coordinator!

When Gerald had gotten commitments from musicians he drew up a schedule that included: the Haw Creek Band, a bluegrass/gospel band of lay people, priests and deacons, and Zilla Kimmel, a Lutheran friend and pianist. Then, the Kellerbergs joined the roster as Sarah, a Suzuki teacher, sang and played her violin and her husband Kevin played his guitar. Sarah also brought her Suzuki students several times to entertain before the Sunday service and to join in leading the worship music. Gerald maintained notebooks for the musicians that contained all the music used for worship at the Advocate, including service music, seasonal songs and hymns.

Gerald also raised up two people among those attending on Sundays to join the music roster when he discovered they could play the piano. One was a man who was unhoused. The other was a woman who was on the work crew and attended the Advocate regularly. She sat down at the piano one day and started playing hymns from the notebook. When Gerald asked her to be one of the Sunday musicians, she told him she didn't have a piano at home for practice. Gerald gave her a keyboard of his own. She came up to Gerald one Sunday with a big smile on her face and said, "My granddaughter who lives with me had never heard me play piano before."

Music wasn't Gerald's only ministry at Church of the Advocate. Rhonda knew that Gerald had computer experience as a business manager and had maintained and operated websites for other businesses. She asked Gerald if he would be responsible for building a new website. Once he designed the new website, he maintained it, along with Facebook and Instagram, providing weekly updates, articles and photos until 2022.

Gerald spoke of Vic Mansfield and Br. John Huebner, saying they were both authentic through and through, and that their simply "being" at Advocate was a blessing. Vic was such a perfect fit because he had been through tragedy in his life. This resonated with the people who trusted Vic as "a man who will walk with us." Gerald was impressed that while Vic was a theologian and biblical scholar, he made the liturgy and message relevant, accessible to the people.

During the Covid lock-down Gerald facilitated an online ministry presence. Tim Ervolina and Dena Whalen would record Sunday meditations. Gerald would then put the meditations into a blog with graphics and music for the website with a link to Facebook and Instagram.

As Gerald reflected on his time at Advocate, he said, "I resonate with Esther in the Old Testament when she was told her position and her proximity to the king 'was for such a time as this' (Esther 4:14) — to save her people. All those years I was in business, working on computers and spreadsheets, and playing music for my own pleasure. Now I come to this juncture and God comes and says that I have learned all this for such a time as this. God was saying to me that even if I was not enough, even if I felt inadequate, he was using me to reach 300 or so people a month. Rhonda, Vic, and Br. John, their steadfastness, gave me a model of how to enter into this new place."

How did God minister to Gerald? He remembers providing music for the Homeless Coalition's annual memorial gathering for those who had died in the past year. During the service, the name of each person who had died was said, followed by the sounding of a chime. Those who had died had been veterans or homeless, with addiction or chronic illness; were estranged from their families. They were all remembered by name. When the litany ended, Gerald intuitively pulled out the song "Let It Be" by the Beatles and everyone joined in singing. "It was right. It took all the names and chimes and prayers and lifted them like sweet incense. I had let the Spirit lead me. Unprepared and flexible is not what I am accustomed to! I found myself in the moment, where the Spirit was."

*Gerald Ashby and Sarah Kellerberg*

*The Haw Creek Band*

*Crew member, Betty, providing music for worship*

# DRAWN BY GOD

*Dena Whalen*

By now, you have read about some of the people who came before me and those whom I worked alongside. They and others gave, and continue to give, generously of their energy, their gifts and their compassion. Church of the Advocate, on the margins of church and society, is a quirky species of church. In some ways it defies organizational stability because of the very nature of the life circumstances of the people who are served and their inability to contribute financially. Its potential for holy, life-changing encounters is profound. However, it is, without a doubt, high-maintenance. To have a firm foundation, it depends on support at all levels – the Diocese, Trinity, area parishes, local agencies, grants, and volunteers. Unlike a typical church, every time the door is opened, the ministry is incomplete without the presence of a nurse and social worker. It finds itself completely vulnerable to the energy and agendas of those who would love it or dismiss it. Much like the people it serves, it can never be self-supporting. Yet, what it proclaims of God's love, Jesus's solidarity, and the Spirit's movements is a powerful and transforming presence among us. Sometimes when people come through the Red Door their lives are changed in big ways. Oftentimes small sincere gestures turn into holy encounters.

When I arrived, I found a liturgy that had been shaped by Vic Mansfield and was artfully presented by Br. John Huebner who had been an elementary school teacher. His teaching skills, paired with his deep devotion to Jesus, created worship that was inviting, calming, and formational. Gerald insured that the worship music was well-organized and relevant. Deacon Tim Ervolina was well-connected with the local food sources and assured that a hot, plentiful meal was prepared every Sunday. When Tim departed, Chef Eric, then Chef Renny and David Robinson followed with the same dedication. They understood the important role that food plays in both physical and spiritual nurturance. The Blue Ridge Service Corps, an intentional community of prayer and action in the Diocese of Western North Carolina, provided the Advocate with interns for two years. This ministry is "dedicated to accompanying our neighbors, many already enacting change and fostering hope in the local community." (blueridgeservicecorps.com) The two young adult interns were a great help with the Good Works! Crew and in the transition between vicars.

During Covid, the Advocate continued every Sunday to provide hot meals to-go, and also delivered sixty-five weekly meals to the respite motel where rooms were provided for infirm and elder unhoused people. The Good Works! Crew held together during Covid and showed up every Sunday to help serve the meals and hand out supplies, and to set up Trinity's Aston Street courtyard for worship. Upon Rhonda's return, the Good Works! Program was renewed and strengthened. The counselors from All Souls Counseling were a lifeline for the crew members and others. Those who gave their time to volunteer were a faithful presence through thick and thin. The Advisory Board members rode the waves of change and strove to articulate a future. Scott White's own advocacy empowered the staff and members of Trinity to embrace every effort made for the Advocate to be true to our call.

When the Covid lock-down was coming to an end, we wondered if our churches and our ministries would be able to re-open successfully. Would people come back? Would we need to radically change the way we did things, the services we offered? One Sunday, while we were still serving food and supplies outside in the Aston Street courtyard, I was given an answer.

Mother Mary, as she is known on the street, came by for her regular Sunday meal and visit. She is a diminutive woman with layers of clothing, long skirts, sturdy black shoes, and a turban on her head. She knows the lay of the land and is respected and protected by the homeless community. Sometimes it's not clear what Mary is talking about and other times she is sharp as a tack. That day I asked her, "What do you think is going to happen when we reopen? Will people come back inside? Do we need to change what we're offering?" She looked off to the side for a moment and then focused her eyes on me and said – firmly – with conviction, "There are plenty of places where the crowds can go. They blow in and out, taking whatever they can get. That's not what the Red Door is for. This place goes deep. There is a peace about it. Folks come in and find the Spirit of God here. Don't go wide. Go deep." Amen, Mary!

As this collection of the narratives of clergy and laity who have shaped the story of the Church of the Advocate comes to a close, I want to contribute two events that deeply affected and instructed me.

# THE SILVER COAT

During the Covid lock-down, a lot of people decided that it was a good time to clean their closets out. Because of this, the Advocate received an *amazing* amount of gently used coats, shoes, clothing, sleeping bags and camping supplies. Since the undercroft of Trinity was not being used, I set up tables and sorted what came in.

One day, as I was sorting donated clothing from giant plastic bags and boxes, I pulled out coats with labels such as Orvis and LL Bean and Brooks Brothers. When I reached in and pulled out a man's full-length coat, I literally stood still for a moment and beheld it. It was the thickest, softest silver-grey cashmere coat I have ever seen. Its label told me that it had been made in Paris.

When it rains, the clothing of those who are sleeping in tents and under bushes gets wet. Without a way to wash or dry their belongings, people end up having to just discard things, especially heavy water-soaked coats and blankets. Then, part of their day's agenda is to go looking for a replacement.

My first thought was, "This gorgeous coat is too good for our coat rack. It would be better to try to sell it and use the money to buy practical items." And I recognized my thought as the words of Judas Iscariot who said the same thing about the expensive nard that a woman used to anoint Jesus' feet.

> Six days before the Passover Jesus came to Bethany, the home of Lazarus, whom he had raised from the dead. ²There they gave a dinner for him. Martha served, and Lazarus was one of those at the table with him. ³Mary took a pound of costly perfume made of pure nard, anointed Jesus' feet, and wiped them with her hair. The house was filled with the fragrance of the perfume. ⁴But Judas Iscariot, one of his disciples (the one who was about to betray him), said, ⁵"Why was this perfume not sold for three hundred denarii and the money given to the poor?" ⁶(He said this not because he cared about the poor, but because he was a thief; he kept the common purse and used to steal what was put into it.) ⁷Jesus said, "Leave her alone. She bought it so that she might keep it for the day of my burial. ⁸You always have the poor with you, but you do not always have me." (John 12:1-11)

I sighed and reached for a hanger and hung it on the rack with the other coats. The next week, one of our regulars, a fifty-year-old man who suffers from dissociative disorder and alcoholism came around the corner wearing the silver cashmere coat that he had chosen from the coat rack. This man often reads scripture and leads the prayers during worship. And his well-trained baritone voice provides music leadership and moving solos.

His face beaming, he said, "Hey, Vicar! How do I look?" He has quite a sense of style and I wasn't surprised that he was the one who chose that coat.

I said, "You look like a million dollars!"

It would not have been a bad thing at all to have placed the coat in an upscale consignment shop and to have gained probably a few hundred dollars with which to buy more practical items. But what I think God wanted me to experience was the replacement of one plumbline for another. This fine article of clothing was created for a certain type of clientele who purchase such finery so as to be in plumb with the context in which they live and the image they strive to uphold.

I witnessed that fine coat die to its old life and be reborn to exist extravagantly in the hands of God who gives it to a beloved one who, yes, needs warmth – and also who needs for someone to look into their eyes, learn their name and offer them love and dignity in a tangible way. And, who also deserves to have a rare moment of delight in having scored such a fine coat!

# DRAWN BY GOD

Each Tuesday a Circle of Prayer and Healing was held at Church of the Advocate, led by Brother John, with music provided by Gerald. It included prayerful reflection upon the lectionary gospel reading for that week, followed by prayer requests, anointing and laying on of hands for healing.

A young man and his female partner had participated in the circle twice. Each time we benefitted from their presence and what they shared. And, he is an exceptional guitarist! One day when he was in the circle, the gospel reading was John 6:35-51.

> [35]Jesus said to them, "I am the bread of life. Whoever comes to me will never be hungry, and whoever believes in me will never be thirsty. [36]But I said to you that you have seen me and yet do not believe. [37]Everything that the Father gives me will come to me, and anyone who comes to me I will never drive away; [38]for I have come down from heaven, not to do my own will, but the will of him who sent me. [39]And this is the will of him who sent me, that I should lose nothing of all that he has given me, but raise it up on the last day. [40]This is indeed the will of my Father, that all who see the Son and believe in him may have eternal life; and I will raise them up on the last day." [41]Then the Jews began to complain about him because he said, "I am the bread that came down from heaven." [42]They were saying, "Is not this Jesus, the son of Joseph, whose father and mother we know? How can he now say, 'I have come down from heaven'?" [43]Jesus answered them, "Do not complain among yourselves. [44]No one can come to me unless drawn by the Father who sent me; and I will raise that person up on the last day. [45]It is written in the prophets, 'And they shall all be taught by God.' Everyone who has heard and learned from the Father comes to me. [46]Not that anyone has seen the Father except the one who is from God; he has seen the Father. [47]Very truly, I tell you, whoever believes has eternal life. [48]I am the bread of life. [49]Your ancestors ate the manna in the wilderness, and they died. [50]This is the bread that comes down from heaven, so that one

may eat of it and not die. [51]I am the living bread that came down from heaven. Whoever eats of this bread will live forever; and the bread that I will give for the life of the world is my flesh."

When it was his turn to name a word or phrase that stood out for him, he said his phrase was "drawn by the Father." Now, the complete verse is: "No one can come to me unless drawn by the Father who sent me." This verse is usually understood to mean that those who come to believe in Jesus are drawn to Jesus because of God's presence in Jesus; that it is not anything sinister in Jesus that draws people to him, but it is God's full presence in Jesus that people find compelling.

This young man took his phrase and went perhaps out of context, but said something that blessed us all.

He said, "God is Creator of all. Everything that exists comes from God's artistry. To think that the Creator of the universe is the artist that drew me into being is amazing to me. Like an artist takes paint to canvas, God has drawn me into being. I have been drawn by God!" These words washed over the circle like a fragrant prophecy that blessed us all.

There were so many times, as others in this narrative have shared, that inspired words and prayers were offered by people, drawn by God, who came through the Red Door. At such times, I've realized that all the while we hoped people would meet Jesus when they came into our midst, it was into our midst that they brought Jesus.

*Mary sharing her wisdom with Dena*

# PHOTOS

*Holy Cross, Tryon, one of several churches who have
provided food and friendship over the years.*

*Susan Sewell delivering the annual gift from Holy Spirit,
Mars Hill. Standing next to her is Matthew Crawford,
the first intern from the Blue Ridge Service Corps.*

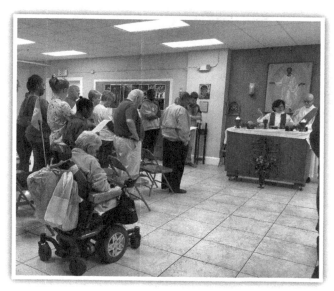

*The altar table - food for the soul*

*The meal tables - food for the body*

# ADAPTING DURING COVID

*Trinity staff and volunteers came to the rescue the first Sunday
of the Covid shut-down. From then on, meals were cheerfully
packaged and served outside throughout the year.*

*Kary Deuel, board member and office manager*

*David Robinson and Liz Minor*

*Chef Eric came to our rescue while his restaurant was closed*

*Chef Renny plating meals for Sunday*

*Clothes poured in from parishes all over the Diocese.*

*Donated clothing*

*Coats always available*

*Support comes in many forms*

Dena Bearl Whalen

# RESOURCES AT THE RED DOOR

*Sole Mate Shoe Closet*

*The Basics for everyday living*

*The Well - First Aid and nursing care*

*Brad Wilson providing nursing care*

# SEASONS AND SACRAMENTS

*Lighting the Advent Candle*

*Friends from Trinity help Advocate decorate for Christmas*

*Prayer and laying on of hands*

*Baptism of Evony and Dereck during Bp. José's visitation*

*Pentecost — Welcoming every tribe and language and people and nation...*

*and species!*

# EPILOGUE

*January, 2024*

It has been a year since the completion of the manuscript. During that time the future of the Red Door wasn't clear. Would it have a new chapter of being opened with new energy and vision, finding its unique voice and place in the larger community of Asheville? Would it continue with a somewhat diminished scope and serve as an outreach of Trinity Church? Was it time to hospice it out, its life span having come to an end?

During a period of discernment, the Bishop, the Rector of Trinity Church, and the Board decided on a new way forward. A search took place and a new Vicar to the Church of the Advocate has taken the call. The Advocate continues to remain distinct as a separate Worshipping Community while Trinity continues to provide, free of charge, the building space and staff support. The leadership studied best practice in terms of the flow of authority and sources of energy. It was determined that the solution best poised for success was to create a full-time clergy position and to call a priest to serve as Assistant Rector at Trinity and Vicar of Church of the Advocate, with the Rector of Trinity will provide oversight and guidance.

Once more, the Advocate has a Vicar, Mike Reardon, who is passionate about the Church's call to serve "the least of these." He brings experience, having previously served as a pastor at the Haywood Street Congregation, and has knowledge of the network of ministries and agencies actively addressing the needs of the unhoused and the underserved in Asheville.

Those who have served at the Advocate through its twenty-five years' presence in Asheville have left their mark. They have worked faithfully, provided great insight, and have expressed hopes and aspirations for the future. New people will be inspired and enthused by the Spirit to converge upon the place with fresh gifts and energy. And, who will come and go through the Red Door? Jesus. In those who go forth and with those who enter.

# ABOUT THE AUTHOR

**Dena Bearl Whalen** has been a priest in the Episcopal Church for 31 years. She has served in various contexts – parish churches, Episcopal schools, an urban cathedral, and diocesan leadership. With a doctorate in congregational development, she has always sought to understand what it takes for any given setting to be a relevant and responsive expression of the good news of God's love in Jesus. Having recently retired, Dena is enjoying family life with her husband Gary, her adult children and grandchildren, a German Shepherd, a Beagle, two rabbits, and her garden. She is involved in interim ministry, establishing a small retreat house to share with others, and soul time with God.

Printed in the United States
by Baker & Taylor Publisher Services